WHEN BRILLIANCE AND MADNESS COLLIDE

Bipolar Disorder Without Boundaries

Ruth Manning, PhD (Meemaw)

Parson's Porch Books

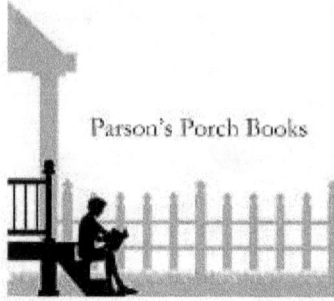

Parson's Porch Books is an imprint of Parson's Porch *&* Company (PP*&*C) in Cleveland, Tennessee. PP*&*C is a self-funded charity which earns money by publishing books of noted authors, representing all genres. Its face and voice is **David Russell Tullock** (dtullock@parsonsporch.com).

Parson's Porch *&* Company *turns books into bread & milk* by sharing its profits with the poor.

www.parsonsporch.com

To my parents,

John and Elsie,
who loved me just the way I am.

The only difference between genius and insanity is that genius has its limits.

—Albert Einstein

Contents

PART III
AMAZING TREK HOME

PART IV
FALLING DOWN THE RABBIT HOLE

PART V
HELP I'VE FALLEN AND I CAN'T GET UP

PART VI
LIFE AFTER PSYCHOSIS

FOREWORD

When Brilliance & Madness Collide is a personal account of Ruth Manning, PhD, who has struggled with bipolar I disorder for the majority of her adult life. Her career path has had a myriad of twists and turns, from serving as founder and CEO of a biotech DNA sequence analysis software company, to working at a US national laboratory, to teaching mathematics as a university professor. These professional successes are interspersed with many hypomanic and manic episodes, over a dozen severe manic psychotic episodes requiring psychiatric hospitalizations, and the personal tragedies of long-time friendships and family keepsakes forever lost to the chaos of a manic or hypomanic state.

This book is partially a memoir and partially a journey inside her mind during a manic psychotic episode that occurred in 2018. Notably, this was the most severe episode of mania and psychosis that she had experienced since 1995. During this period, Ruth went five days without food or sleep, which is very dangerous for a 67-year-old diabetic and led to twenty pounds of unintentional weight loss. She experienced numerous hallucinations, psychoses, and tangential connections that nearly resulted in a house fire, which she later chronicled in multiple notebooks while still hypomanic and recovering in a psychiatric hospital.

Her story is separated into six parts that are recounted chronologically—with Parts III, IV, and V reflecting her hypomanic (nonhospitalized), manic (nonhospitalized), and manic-hypomanic (hospitalized) states, respectively. The book also includes some of the clinical documentation of her psychiatric hospitalization, providing an objective measure of her progress and recovery each day. Throughout the book, Ruth frequently refers to her mental wellness using Meemaw1 (normal), Meemaw2 (hypomanic), and Meemaw3 (manic) descriptors, though the exact lines between each state may blur or may exist concurrently. She defines this concurrency as ontological simultaneity. It is perhaps most evident in Part II of her book, where it can be difficult to see where some of her more subtle delusions and experiences blend with her Meemaw1 state.

When she enters manic and hypomanic states, Ruth will often gain religious undertones that drive her actions, thoughts, and hallucinations. This is true to her being, just as much as her desire to help others or give away personal possessions is ingrained. As one reads through the middle and later sections of this book, those undertones will become more pronounced—subtly at first, then unmistakable. Reading this book provides a journey into the mind of a person with type I bipolar disorder, with each tangential connection and hallucination described in detail.

The descriptors she uses for her mental wellness are well known to me, as I grew up seeing them firsthand. As one of her two children, we spent every other day at a different parent's house and needed to track what weekend of the month it was to know which bus to ride. Travel plans with Mom were always restricted unless another adult who knew her well was also in tow. Since this was all we knew as children, we adapted to this level of responsibility as if it was a normal state of affairs. That plan worked well for about a decade until a particularly severe psychotic episode and hospitalization in 1995 jarred us into the reality of how far her mental health disorder could go.

The mere fact that we were changing houses every day was what clued our dad into Mom's severe psychosis in 1995, leading to early intervention and hospitalization. There's something to be said about having two children arrive in tears, having just said goodbye forever to their mom, thinking it was actually the end of the world and that she needed to go to Omaha, Nebraska to preach the gospel. That was quite the awakening into adulthood. Having also witnessed Mom's psychosis in 2018 (with many episodes in between), and in my current role as an emergency physician caring for patients with mental health emergencies, I understand why a psychiatrist in the 1980s had told Mom that her bipolar disorder was "the second worst case he had ever seen."

But just as well as I have seen her at her least emotionally stable states, that is not my mom. Most of the time, we trust her to watch our kids unattended. She never used illicit drugs, and she always made a point of keeping stable housing despite her career swaps and later reliance on disability services. Mom is kind, dedicated, and driven; but compassion is her strongest quality by far. This trait escalates considerably when she enters a manic or hypomanic state, to the point where she has given away many cherished family keepsakes, her car, and even one of her companies.

Even without manic features, Mom's empathy shines through. She will go the extra mile to help others, particularly those who are in unstable and disadvantaged positions. Over the years, we've had people stay at our house for months on end while they seek to get their bearings, such as a family who immigrated to be near their son and who only spoke Filipino and Spanish when they first arrived in the US. Her work to elevate disadvantaged and minority students also exemplifies this well. Growing up in her house—despite the occasional psychotic setbacks—helping others from underserved walks of life was the norm, not the exception.

Ruth Manning's journey has been an emotional rollercoaster. Her book is written to exemplify how success, failure, mania, and psychosis can occur in tandem. It is written to show the perspective of a person who must constantly be mindful of her mental wellness and must bounce back from each inevitable setback. It is written to let others with mental health disorders know that they are not alone and that they can still live a successful life despite their challenges and struggles. To their friends, family members, and loved ones, it is written to provide context and let them experience what it's like to be in a psychotic state happening outside of their control.

Mom, thank you for sharing your life's story. I'm proud of you.

Love,
—John Manning, MD

PREFACE

The highest hurdle I had to jump to write *Brilliance and Madness* was not the obvious vulnerability of social stigma because I use my real name. Rather, it was my fear of rejection, perhaps the most negative trigger influencing my emotional/bipolar state, that will inevitably come from readers from both extremes of the spectrum of religious beliefs and systems. Some might focus on my evangelical Christian faith upbringing, while others, ironically, might consider some parts of the book to border on heresy or blasphemy.

I discussed this quandary with my creative writing mentor, Don Williams—author, columnist, and founding editor of the anthology, *New Millennium Writings*—who counseled me to follow Ernest Hemingway's advice. In his memoir, *A Moveable Feast*, Hemingway writes introspectively about creative pause:

> *All you have to do is write one true sentence. Write the truest sentence that you know.*

In *Brilliance and Madness*, I take TRUTH to another level. Some of my spiritual experiences in 2017–18 connected tangentially to my psychotic state in 2018, so I included many of the details, writing truthfully from my own perspective…with all delusions and illusions intact.

My journey shows a mind that was slowly spiraling out of control while I still believed I was in a baseline state. My imaginings and delusions can be subtle. Sometimes it's difficult to distinguish what is real. Just like in my dreams, while sleeping, they can draw upon anything from early childhood experiences to current events, strung together in no particular order or logic.

My beliefs and faith are expressed throughout this book to illuminate my story, not to try to convince others what to believe. I am certainly not advising people to ignore medical science! I clearly acknowledge that my medical treatment is crucial to living well with bipolar disorder, and when I stopped taking my medications in mid-2018, before my extreme psychotic episode—because I thought I was healed and didn't need them—that was part of what propelled me into a manic psychosis.

Just as my moods have fluctuated between mania and depression, my devotion to my Christian faith has sometimes wavered, somewhere between hedonistic and sanctimonious, usually influenced by my mental health at the time. My misguided, overzealous, obsession with converting an atheist friend to Christianity finally destroyed our close friendship of twenty-eight years and led to the rejection that brought about my psychosis in mid-2018.

I include my bipolar management plan to *develop coping strategies and a lifestyle that minimize my bipolar symptoms*—including, maintaining a regular daily schedule and routine with balance and structure (work, eating, sleep, exercise, Bible study, prayer, etc.); self-monitoring (watching for potential problems and relapses); asking family and friends to help monitor my bipolar symptoms and behavior; and always taking my mental health medications as prescribed by a medical professional.

One of the underlying themes of *Brilliance and Madness* is how my spiritual health helps me cope with my serious mental health problems, much like others with lived experience might use exercise, private or group therapy, meditation, etc. I imagine this book will probably speak strongly to other Christians who struggle with mental health issues and reveal what role their faith plays (or doesn't) in the illness, hopefully helping them to reconcile both, as I have done.

I respect the diversity of all faith traditions and value the experiences of people who are different from me. For the sake of inclusion, I hope all readers can put aside their personal beliefs and biases and see this book as it is intended—to tell the *truth* about my lived experience during the escalation from baseline in early 2017 through the progression of stages of mania in 2017–18, culminating in full-blown psychosis in mid-2018, and my post-psychosis experiences in late 2018–21, including my mental/emotional reactions to COVID-19.

—Ruth Manning, 2023

PROLOGUE

I knew little about bipolar I disorder before Ruth Manning approached me about doing a developmental edit on her memoir, *When Brilliance and Madness Collide*. Ruth came to me because I specialize in working on books about healing from illness, trauma, and loss, and because I specialize in books that are "weird." She assured me that her memoir was both, and after reading her brief description, I was intrigued. Three different robot narrators and an in-depth, firsthand account of a psychotic episode…how could I resist? I checked out Ruth's website, ruthforthebroken.org, and discovered a comprehensive, compassionate site full of information, advice, and resources for people dealing with a variety of mental health diseases and disorders. This was obviously an author who knew how to do research, how to write, and, perhaps most compellingly, an author who cared deeply about helping others living with mental illness or caring for a loved one with mental illness. I knew this was a project I wanted to help bring into the world.

As I went through the manuscript, I laughed out loud, I teared up…and I learned a lot. There are many wonderful books and online resources out there about mental illnesses and about bipolar disorder in particular. But this book offers a unique perspective by bringing the reader inside the head of a person experiencing mania, paranoia, and psychosis. By taking copious notes during an acute psychotic episode in 2018, Ruth was able, in its aftermath, to reconstruct what she was thinking and doing and write it down in a format that is both fascinating and entertaining.

This in-depth account sheds light on an often-misunderstood disorder. Before reading this book, if someone had said "psychosis," I would have imagined an extremely violent individual, stripped of all social conditioning and completely out of control and out of touch with themselves. *When Brilliance and Madness Collide* shows a different aspect of psychosis: an individual compulsively doing good deeds for others and obsessing about how to make the world better. Readers will come away from this account with a more nuanced understanding of the different forms psychosis can take and deeper insight into the state of mind of a person experiencing psychosis.

I was fascinated to see how the imaginings/delusions during the psychotic episode sometimes mirror the types of make-believe games and stories that children make up (for example, the author's subdivision was Eden, or Heaven, or Jerusalem, and different places in the subdivision represented different places in these imaginings). It's almost as if the mind in a psychotic state taps into the person's childhood sense of reality, when make-believe could feel real, before the child's sense of "concrete reality" was fully formed. The author's psychotic delusions also resemble dreams in their sense of "logic" and organization, as if, perhaps, the unconscious mind that is responsible for dreams takes over one's waking life during psychosis. The chapters that introduce and frame the psychotic episode allow readers to get to know the author, so we see how the delusions she experienced during the episode related to the rest of her life and interests. The creative way Ruth has written about the experiences in these chapters allows a reader who doesn't suffer from bipolar disorder to relate in some way to the reality she was living in, since everyone dreams, and everyone remembers what it was like to be a child, when the border between reality and imagination was thinner—at least, I hope everyone remembers that feeling!

An account like the one you are about to read offers those of us who do not live with mental illness a way to relate to and understand, at least in some small way, those who do. This more personal understanding cultivates compassion—the essential human trait that allows us to care for one another. This memoir is indeed a "wild ride," entertaining and enlightening, which succeeds in its mission to educate and inspire readers to change how we think about and care for those living with mental illness.

Buckle up!

Deborah K. Steinberg
San Francisco, 2023

INTRODUCTION

Bipolar-Life

The stigma of mental illness is when your psychological state defines your identity; when people see you as flawed and incompetent; when you are invisible to others; or when people see your suffering but blame you for it. It is the unwanted shadow of a person, produced when a society casts a certain light on human differences.

—Roy Richard Grinker, *Nobody's Normal: How Culture Created the Stigma of Mental Illness*

On June 4, 2018, my neighbors Rick and Judy found me naked, lying on the floor in my den, ostensibly attempting to insert an extended-reach grabber tool into my vagina. They called my daughter Megan and 911.

I remember being carried out of my house on a gurney and put into an ambulance. We whizzed by the trees which enveloped the highway. I recognized the blaring sounds of the wailing siren and felt the stick of a needle, but I didn't remember anything more until sometime after I was transported to University General Hospital, about two and a half miles away. The next thing I recall was being in an isolation room, where I remained on a gurney until I could be transferred to a locked holding room.

Later, the University General Hospital staff told my son, Elijah, that sometime during my temporary bipolar blackout, when I was not aware of what was taking place and had no memory of it, I had sucker punched a police officer in the face, knocking his glasses to the ground, and then tried to kiss him on the mouth as he bent over to pick them up. I don't think I was tased, though I probably should have been. This incident was not recorded in my medical records, so I don't know any more specific details. I must have been experiencing superhuman strength, as I had in several of my prior psychotic episodes. The most recent one before this had been in 1995.

Superhuman strength (also called hysterical strength) refers to short periods of increased strength beyond what is believed to be the normal or natural human range and is sometimes manifested during psychosis or a state of extreme agitation and delirium. It's believed to be caused by a rush of the hormone adrenaline and triggered by the body's stress response.

Later that week, I was transferred to Broadmoor, a psychiatric hospital over an hour's drive away. After I returned home, I called the police department and apologized. The police officer I talked to had obviously heard the story. He told me to not worry about it; it was all in a day's work. However, I doubt if they often encounter half-naked, pantyless, crazed, older women who jab them in their faces and then try to kiss them!

I was first diagnosed with bipolar disorder in December 1982 after a full-blown psychotic manic episode. Because of this psychosis and my subsequent hospitalization, I fall into the category of bipolar I disorder.

Bipolar disorder (sometimes called manic depression) is a disease of the brain usually characterized by dramatic changes in mood, thinking, behavior, and activity levels. This mood disorder can be both limiting and debilitating for an individual's personal, social, and professional life.

Following my first psychotic experience in 1982, a psychiatrist informed me that the episode was the second-worst case he had ever witnessed. I neither put that on my resume nor wore it as a badge of honor. He must not have seen many cases, because psychoses leading to some of my dozen or so subsequent psychiatric hospitalizations took bizarreness to a whole new level!

Though I can write objectively about my mental illness—and even recognize the humor in some of the things it's caused me to do—bipolar disorder has taken a devastating toll on me. For a long time, I identified myself with the disease: "I *am* bipolar." My diagnosis and sometimes psychosis invaded my everyday life, transcending all my other roles: bipolar mother of two; bipolar grandmother (Meemaw) of four; bipolar founder and CEO of a biotech software company that licensed, developed, and marketed DNA sequence analysis software worldwide; bipolar national laboratory scientist; bipolar computing consultant for some of the fastest supercomputers in the world; bipolar market analyst for a small investment startup for which I'm a cofounder; bipolar university, community college, and HBCU mathematics professor, and more.

My convoluted career path was definitely related to the mania of my bipolar disorder. Once, I had four part-time technical consulting jobs simultaneously! Still, it's a conundrum to explain how I could have been so successful in my career if you compare that timeline side by side with my mental health history.

The goal of this book is to provide an overview of what the *ordinary life* of a person with bipolar disorder might look like, as well as an in-depth perspective on what a person with bipolar disorder experiences during a psychotic episode through a detailed account of the mental breakdown I had in 2018.

A linear spectrum for bipolar disorder is labeled as extreme mania (psychosis), moderate mania, hypomania (mild mania), normal mood (baseline), mild depression, moderate depression, and severe depression. In this book, I will focus on the manic side of this spectrum. Mania has always been the more serious and predominant mood disorder for me. Before my mother passed away in 1997, I hadn't been depressed enough to notice.

I can usually tell when I'm headed toward extreme bipolar mania before it gets out of control. When I'm still able to recognize the warning signs, I alert friends and family to monitor me closely before I reach a point of no return.

The symptoms can vary among patients, but for me, it usually begins with unpredictable mood changes (increased anxiety or elevated mood), poor judgment, and excessive talking. As the illness progresses, I experience periods of extreme energy, euphoria, and occasional grandiose ideas about myself. Sometimes I have some combination of disorganized speech, inability to focus, insomnia, hypersexuality, profligate spending, obsessing over things, or overestimation of my abilities. My thoughts become disconnected and flighty. My mind feels as though it's racing. Sometimes I become irritable. I require less sleep. As severe mania progresses to psychosis, my thinking becomes delusional, and I eventually lose all touch with reality.

At the early stages of moderate to extreme mania, it can feel like my skin is crawling. Sometimes I have a peculiar, pungent odor coming from my armpits, though I've never heard another patient with bipolar mania complain of this. It might be caused by a fatty type of sweat produced from the apocrine gland in response to stress. My ex-husband Steve insisted it was an indicator of an impending psychotic manic episode (or at least moderate mania).

This is the best way I can describe what it feels like before my psychosis reaches the point of no return. Imagine the moment right before Dr. Bruce Banner's head begins to swell, while he is *hulking out* in *The Incredible Hulk* TV series. At a single point in time, it feels like *something* snaps in my brain. Then it's too late to turn back the hands of time.

Researchers continue to study this complex neurological illness. They want to know more about how neurotransmitters (chemical messengers in the brain) communicate with other parts of the brain and the nervous system. Though there are no definitive answers, scientists agree that bipolar disorder is a biochemical, neurological disorder, and that genetic and environmental factors can play a role.

In 1972, I coined the phrase "ontological simultaneity"—simultaneously being. I can best define it by giving an example: a painting of a woman painting a picture of a woman painting a picture of a woman painting a picture of...ad infinitum. I can think of no better way to describe the brilliance and madness of my wild bipolar ride.

The writing style and composition of this book reflect the unique way I perceive and process information and experiences in these states of ontological simultaneity. I have imagined three distinct robots—Meemaw1, Meemaw2, and Meemaw3—to represent and write about my moods, behaviors, and experiences at different levels of mania. Because of my background in computing and technology, robots are a natural metaphor for me to use to describe my experiences.

I've employed these robot narrators so readers can get into the mind of a person with bipolar disorder and peek behind the curtain to see what's invisible to the observer. What we're thinking and what you think we're thinking are often worlds apart.

I tend to suppress my painful emotions of embarrassment, shame, rejection, hurt feelings, sadness, anger, and social exclusion. Dealing with such issues directly has always been difficult for me, so I hide behind the facades of wit and satire. I sometimes make light of many of my outlandish experiences. Using the robot narrators allowed me to achieve enough distance from events to write about them without feeling overwhelmed by difficult emotions.

Meemaw1 represents as close to a normal mood (baseline) as I ever get and ranges somewhere between normal mood and hypomania. Hypomania is a milder version of mania that lasts for a short period, sometimes only a few days.

Meemaw2 ranges from hypomania through all stages of moderate mania.

Meemaw3 begins at the upper level of moderate mania, cycles through extreme mania (psychosis), and begins the process of cycling back down to moderate mania.

In this book, only robots Meemaw1 and Meemaw2 are narrators. For the most part, Meemaw3 is just a psychotic performer whose actions are reported by Meemaw2.

Parts I and VI of this book were written by robot Meemaw1 to frame the 2018 psychotic episode in the larger context of the rest of my life.

Part II, which chronicles the events in 2017 and the first half of 2018 leading to my 2018 psychotic episode, was originally written by Meemaw2, but edits and additions were made later by Meemaw1. Parts III, IV, and V of this book, which record the episode itself and my subsequent recovery, were written by robot Meemaw2, with a few edits made later by Meemaw1— mainly to cut material. The experiences related in Part II are attributable either to robot Meemaw1 or Meemaw2, while Parts III, IV, and V describe the moods and actions of Meemaw3 exclusively.

In Part II, sometimes I couldn't distinguish whether a mood or activity belonged to Meemaw1 or Meemaw2. Many times, professionals, friends, and family also fail to identify these distinctions. This is complicated because the progression of moods along the bipolar disorder spectrum is not always successive and can alternate back and forth with no clear time demarcations.

I hope readers will be able to experience what it's like to have bipolar disorder by the way the Meemaw2 sections of the book are written. Meemaw2 wrote about Meemaw3 soon after I returned from a mental hospital in 2018. I had kept receipts and made copious notes while at the hospital, but I didn't remember the linear sequences of the chaotic events. In the Meemaw2 stage following my hospital stay, I was able to recall a series of similar events and collect them into adventures, which I chose to describe as video or virtual reality games, board games, TV game shows, soap operas, plays, etc. My choices of representations reflect my age, interests, and experiences, as well as Meemaw2's creative way of thinking.

My psychosis in 2018 gradually increased in intensity. The changes in the way I thought about and perceived my environment were arbitrary. There were distinct sets of random themes in which my psychotic (delusional) manifestations appeared to vacillate backward and forward in time. Meemaw3 would cycle between sets of ad hoc activities in no particular order or frequency. During the darkest periods of the psychosis, I would imagine or sense the presence of people and voices that were not there.

Though the chapters chronicling the events of the acute phase of the 2018 psychotic episode are distinct, thanks to Meemaw2's organization of the memories into narratives, I did not experience them in any specific order, frequency, or predictability.

Each segment of Meemaw2's narrative of the psychotic episode describes the background, setting, rules, or other appropriate documentation that enables the reader to participate in the behind-the-scenes reasoning and actions of a psychotic mind. These are thoughts and reflections the psychiatrist, psychologist, family, friends, and casual observers and readers have no way of knowing or understanding. They usually only see small snapshots of what's actually taking place in the psychotic patient's mind.

In Part V, which chronicles my stay in the psychiatric hospital, I include notes made by doctors and nurses in my medical chart. These notes introduce an additional narrative voice that is more detached and objective than any of the Meemaw robot narrators. The medical voice is an outside, extremely unbiased one that contrasts with the up-close-and-personal account of events as written by Meemaw2.

The medical notes tell the story of my recovery during my hospitalization in specialized language that is meaningful to medical professionals but may be opaque to readers unfamiliar with this language. A glossary of medical terms and abbreviations that appear in these notes is included as an appendix to help readers decipher them.

I wrote the account of my 2018 psychosis first, as Meemaw2, in a manic fury during the six weeks following my return from the psychiatric hospital. I had grandiose notions. I thought this was to be the best book ever written about bipolar psychosis, because it was so precise and comprehensive. I even measured the thickness of the wood used to make my baby doll cradle! I was dreaming of co-authors, editors, agents, publishers, book signings…the whole nine yards. I was even thinking about how money is not that important to me. What charities would I support with all the profits?

Then reality set in. My friend Rachel, who is a highly regarded published writer, read the first fifty pages of Part IV and gave it a less than stellar review. But later, she read more pages a couple of times and gave me valuable feedback about how I could make this into a book that people would want to read. So, after quarantine and self-isolation, alone in my apartment for most of 2020, I decided to finish it. I had already made a new website and two new blogs and had run out of any more procrastination projects.

Those with lived experience and their families and friends are often reluctant to discuss mental illness or reach out for help because of denial, embarrassment, or lack of understanding. Education and transparency are the best ways to combat this stigma.

My hope is that my story will help family, friends, colleagues, and the public to love, understand, and provide care and protection for people who have a mental health condition. Improved healthcare, shelters, group homes, laws, police training, and education about how to recognize the symptoms of depression, mania, and psychosis would be a start. More information is provided in my blog: www.ruthforthebroken.org.

PART I

MY WILD RIDE

Meemaw1

1951–2016

A Family Legacy

If you're going to live, leave a legacy. Make a mark on the world that can't be erased.

—Maya Angelou

Early Years

I was born in 1951 and grew up cultivating crops and raising livestock on a small, rural farm in East Tennessee with my two brothers and our father and mother. My paternal grandparents were born in the 1860s and had passed away long before I was born. After my father died in 1959, my maternal grandparents, Mammaw and Pappy, stepped in and played an important role in my childhood development. They lived about three miles away. We visited them every day.

Mammaw taught me how to make biscuits, lattice cherry pies, and imparted any other culinary skills I might have acquired. These skills have long gone by the wayside. She also taught me how to make cross-stitched aprons and assisted Mom in helping me make dresses, blouses, and skirts. All of my clothes, including my wedding dress, were homemade by one of the three of us until after I married.

Each year, we butchered one of our steers and slaughtered a hog to provide meat for my grandparents and us. We froze the roasts, steaks, other cuts of beef, and the meat we ground for hamburgers. Our upright freezer also contained homemade sausage, pork chops, ribs, and pork steaks. We hung the salted hams in the smokehouse out back. Though we rendered lard from the hog to use in cooking, we didn't make chitlins (from the large intestine) or souse meat (made from various other leftover parts of the pig, including feet, head, ears, and tail—pretty much everything but the squeal). Some people consider souse meat a delicacy.

We grew our own food and canned or froze the vegetables, fruits, and jellies and jams we made. I chose canning, freezing, and sewing as my 4-H club projects. Mom was a perfectionist. I had to take out many seams and do them over again if, upon inspection, she didn't think the garment would win a blue ribbon at the county fair, whether I entered it into a contest or not.

Dad had bought us a $25 upright piano the year he died. I took piano lessons from the third grade through my senior year of high school, but I didn't become accomplished like my brother. I did teach piano during my high school years and even played Peter Nero's arrangement of "Mountain

9

Greenery" at a statewide convention in Nashville for the Future Teachers of America Association. I'm sure my rendition would've made Peter cringe.

One of Mom's sisters and her husband also sort of adopted my brothers and me. They were excellent role models. They owned a dirt racetrack (where I worked in the concessions stand as a teenager) and a gas station (where I assisted with bookkeeping, beginning when I was in the sixth grade). This gave me an early exposure to entrepreneurship.

I was voted "Most Likely to Succeed" female by my high school peers. I would've been a valedictorian of my class had I not been disqualified after I entered the nearby land-grant university in their Early Admissions Program after making a qualifying score on my ACT. I stayed in high school the first half of my senior year because I had been elected president of the Future Homemakers of America, Beta Club, and Future Teachers of America. I reasoned that I didn't want to let them down, but my desire to be near my boyfriend, my high school sweetheart who was already at the university, won out and I attended the university for the last half of my senior year.

I married my high school sweetheart in 1969, soon after I graduated, and we were together until 1981. I earned a PhD in mathematics in 1979 and taught university courses, ranging from fundamentals, calculus, abstract algebra, differential equations, and advanced calculus, at a nearby university from 1976 to 1978. Then, I worked on optimizing scientific computer programs for some of the world's fastest supercomputers from 1979 to 1989.

So far, successful by most standards? However, looming from my past were early indicators of my mental illness that were not noticed or diagnosed. Mom did recognize that I was *different.*

She would say I often "flew off the handle" like her sister Ola. She'd even tell me that if I didn't quit "acting *that* way," I would get sick like my dad before I was twenty. I remember my relief after my twentieth birthday. I made it!

In my late twenties, I became loquacious and began experiencing unpredictable changes in mood and reckless judgment. These symptoms of mental illness were heightened by periods of high energy, occasional exaggerated beliefs about myself and my abilities, and exhilaration, especially near the end of my first marriage in 1981. Had these symptoms been diagnosed and treated earlier, my first psychotic episode at age 31 might have been preventable.

That first psychotic episode also might have been easier to foresee if more information had been available about the genetic component of bipolar disorder at that time. For there was certainly evidence of mental illness in my father's family.

10

Genetic Predisposition

In June 1905, Uncle George's legs were severed when he tried to hobo a train, and he died. He was thirteen years old. George was going to meet his two older brothers, Joseph and Robert (ages fourteen and fifteen, respectively), who were coming home to Middlesboro from working in the coal mines of Kentucky.

I was told Grandma Sallie—my dad's mother—had a nervous breakdown (as we would call a psychotic episode back then) when George died. Presumably this was her only severe mental illness episode. Since our family kept mental illness hush-hush, I don't know any details about her experience. George was her third child, and his sister Edna (the eleventh of seventeen children) was only two months old at the time of Grandma Sallie's breakdown. I'm sure the effects of postpartum and birthing her first eleven children over a span of just sixteen years took their toll, too. Grandpa Henry died in 1919 during the Spanish flu pandemic, but there's no oral history about her reaction to his death.

Bipolar disorder is one of the most heritable of mental illnesses, but decoding its genetic basis has been scientifically challenging. The paternal side of my family has a genetic history of mental illness, notably bipolar disorder, though before the 1950s it was labeled as schizophrenia. Since my father—the fifteenth of Grandma Sallie's seventeen children—and some of his siblings were hospitalized with psychoses, I used to muse that our family would be a good candidate for genetic familial studies, though I never could have convinced any of my family members to permit their loved ones to be exhumed.

Dad's first psychotic episode occurred in 1943 during World War II, while he was deployed in New Guinea in the Southwest Pacific. Though he had a genetic predisposition, I believe the psychological stresses of war pushed him over the edge. Dad's responsibility was to repair guns—specifically, a type of airplane machine gun. He believed that he had devised a way to make the machine gun fire more rounds per minute, but he wasn't able to convince his superiors that his idea would work. The problem may have been Army bureaucracy, or simply that retooling to change the design would have caused too many problems. Or it may have been that increasing the rate of fire would create more heat than the gun could handle long-term.

Whatever the reasons, his frustration and feelings of rejection probably contributed to his breakdown.

Recently, I found a copy of his honorable medical discharge certificate from the Army. All of my relatives are deceased who might have known any details about his recovery from this first breakdown, including the treatment he received and how long it took him to recover.

11

During Dad's first episode, while serving in the Army, his vocal cords were injured. Mom told my older brother that at some point they were having trouble restraining him in the hospital, and an orderly or nurse grabbed him in a choke hold from behind to try to control him. The ensuing struggle damaged his vocal cord muscles, and after that, he couldn't talk above a whisper. My brothers and I never heard him speak with a natural voice.

I think he might have been experiencing superhuman strength, as has been my experience during some of my extreme manic psychotic episodes.

Dad only had two more confirmed psychotic episodes, in 1949–50 and 1955, though he might have had some early symptoms before the stroke and coronary thrombosis that caused his death in 1959. In contrast, I've had more than a dozen severe psychotic manic episodes, mostly between 1982 and 1990, but also in 1995 and 2018.

Dad received Electroconvulsive Therapy (ECT) while at a VA hospital in 1955. We just called them shock treatments at the time. As a child, it made me angry to know they'd done that cruel and inhumane thing to him. In later years, I feared that I might be given such treatments myself. When I watched the movie *One Flew Over the Cuckoo's Nest*, it felt all too real to me. I had to leave the room when Jack Nicholson's character received ECT.

Dad's diagnosis was always schizophrenia. He had no access to psychiatrists or psychologists in our small town, so his family physician kept him medicated with a high dose of Thorazine, an antipsychotic medication often used to treat schizophrenia. I remember him being tired all the time after working hard on the farm. In the evenings, when he wasn't reading his Bible or holding one or two of his children on his lap or playing with us, he would catnap in his recliner. His drowsiness could have been a side effect of his medication. But I don't recall him trembling or having shaky hands, which are also side effects of Thorazine.

Dad read his Bible a lot, and his delusions often took on religious themes. My older brother told me that one time Dad thought he was Simon Peter, and my brother was Baby Jesus. An aunt told me about a time when Dad thought he was Jesus and peed in a bucket in the kitchen of an old house on our farm (where he was staying to protect the rest of our family during his psychosis). She said he brought the bucket to the room where three of his brothers were sitting and offered to wash their feet. I don't know how the incident ended, but I presume they thwarted that one!

Jesus Washes His Disciples' Feet
Jesus knew that the Father had given him authority over everything and that he had come from God and would return to God. So he got up from the table, took off his

12

robe, wrapped a towel around his waist, and poured water into a basin. Then he began to wash the disciples' feet, drying them with the towel he had around him (John 13:3-5 Holy Bible, New Living Translation [NLT]).

Many people thought the reason Dad would have these episodes was that he was too religious. I'm sure he read the Bible even more when he was about to become psychotic, but had he been a historian, he might have read history books and thought he was Napoleon or other important historical figures.

Some of my family members also think I tend to get sick because of my religious bent. But it's all about cause and effect. It's because of my love for Jesus that I sometimes experience Christian motifs during my episodes. But my relationship with God does not cause me to get sick. Sometimes I think this has been a stumbling block to faith for some of my relatives. They're afraid that if they're too religious, they might have a nervous breakdown.

I come from a long line of Protestant Christians. Mom and her parents were charter members of Friendship Missionary Baptist Church. From infancy on, Mom took my brothers and me to church every time the doors were opened. That's where I became well grounded in the truths and precepts of the Bible.

Though Dad's father, Grandpa Henry, had been a Pentecostal Holiness preacher, Dad had quit attending church sometime before I was born, mostly because of his health. But the Christian values of faith, love, and forgiveness that he imparted to me, and our shared love for reading the Bible, remain a treasured connection to him. Each morning and evening, when we went to the barn to feed or see about our cattle, he would kneel with me on his hands and knees on the manure dirt barn floor and pray lengthy prayers to God. He always began with "Holy! Righteous! Heavenly Father!"

Both of my parents taught me by example to follow God's two greatest commandments—to love God above all else and to love others as myself. I responded to God's invitation to be a follower of Jesus Christ at age ten.

But while much of what our parents impart to us is learned, much is also inherited, as is the case with bipolar I disorder in my family. I have examples of extreme mental illness psychoses spanning three of my paternal generations—perhaps there were others before Grandma Sallie. It will be interesting to see what light future scientific research sheds on the genetic component of this disorder.

Brilliance and Madness

In madness, I thought I was the most important person in the world.

—John Forbes Nash Jr.

Insanity

In October 1982, I married Steve, a brilliant, successful engineer/inventor/entrepreneur. By the end of that year, I'd landed in a psych ward in North Palm Beach because a shower head told me to go to the Intracoastal Waterway and scream when I saw a small plane overhead to alert my husband of my whereabouts...only problem was, the shower head forgot to tell me to put on some clothes!

Like my dad, I also received a diagnosis of schizophrenia. Similar to him, there were several times, when I was psychotic, that I had superhuman strength, making me difficult to control. It took two or three men to restrain me while a nurse injected me with a tranquilizing shot of Thorazine.

Steve arrived later that evening and insisted I be discharged. He flew me back to Knoxville that night in a rented single-engine Cessna. My diagnosis was changed to bipolar I disorder, and I was prescribed lithium, which was cheap and readily available. Lithium was not approved by the United States Food and Drug Administration (FDA) for the treatment of bipolar disorder until 1970, though it had been widely used in other parts of the world for quite some time. So Dad couldn't have benefited from lithium therapy.

My psychotic behavior didn't end with the first hospitalization. I became psychotic again after the birth of our first child, Megan, in 1983. Steve had to bring her home from the hospital without me. The psychiatrist had promised to come to the hospital and put me back on lithium after her birth. I was furious that he hadn't! With superhuman strength, I jumped high off the floor and tried to *kick him where it hurts,* as Mom would say (she didn't know the word *cojones*). He had me strapped to a gurney in no time flat, and I believe he left me there for a good while. Who could blame him?

The psychiatric hospital gave me weekend passes to visit Megan until my mental health improved enough to assist her grandmothers with her care.

In 1984, my psychiatrist tried to convince us to abort our son, Elijah, because of my severe manic psychotic episode after Megan was born the year before. We didn't, and I didn't experience a manic episode after he was born in 1985. Nonetheless, I averaged one psychotic episode per year during our eight-year marriage.

During extreme bipolar psychotic episodes, I experienced delusions with similar themes to the ones Dad had, especially religious ones. One time, Steve saved my life by sprinting to the porch to flip the main switch in the circuit box when he heard both the hairdryer and water running in a locked bathroom. It would have been ruled a suicide. How could anyone have known what was going on inside my brain? I thought I was Jesus and, therefore, invincible.

Though Dad's diagnosis was always schizophrenia, I think he was misdiagnosed, as I was in 1982. Psychosis symptoms are similar for both diagnoses. Even during non-psychotic times, more than 70 percent of people with schizophrenia have visual hallucinations[1] and/or hear voices.[2] Though Dad and I both had delusions (false beliefs) and hallucinations (feelings or impressions that something imagined is real) during our psychoses, neither of us had visual or auditory hallucinations during ordinary times.

During my psychiatric hospital stays, I've observed schizophrenic patients having conversations with multiple people (invisible to me), supplying the dialogue for each. One man carried on a heated three-way conversation about whether he had called someone a *son of a bitch.* The patient was seated at a dining table. A *friend* was standing, and *another* was seated at an adjacent table. The conversation seemed so real; I thought they would come to blows![3]

For me, during psychosis, there's a fine line between what is a delusion versus a hallucination. During my psychotic episode in 2018, I sometimes believed I was talking to people who weren't there. If I were truly schizophrenic, I think it's likely I would have heard and seen these imaginary people and believed they were in the room with me. However, though I sensed their presence and imagined what they were thinking or saying, I never actually heard their voices or saw things or people that didn't exist.

For example, in 2018, I remember conveying a message to Elijah without actually seeing him. I don't remember how I did that—maybe through a third party, whom I also did not see. I consider that experience to be a delusion rather than a hallucination, since my visual and auditory senses were not engaged. I also remember thinking that it was raining, but I believe the rain was real.

---

[1]https://www.ncbi.nlm.nih.gov/pmc/articles/PMC3105559/
[2]https://ww.ncbi.nlm.nih.gov/pmc/articles/PMC2525988
[3]The book *A Beautiful Mind* by Sylvia Nassar and the subsequent movie are based on the life of the American mathematician, John Forbes Nash Jr., a Nobel Laureate in Economics—perhaps the most famous person with schizophrenia of our time. The imaginary characters in the movie enabled me to get inside the mind of Dr. Nash. At first, I couldn't tell which characters were the imaginary ones.

Adventures in Supercomputing

During the 1980s, when I experienced the majority of my extreme manic psychotic episodes, I was also a supercomputing consultant, teaching classes nationwide and optimizing scientific computer codes to run faster on my company's computers than those of our competitors. We often outperformed on benchmarks, but rarely won the contracts. Our main competitor had better and more popular computers; benchmarking was more of a competition between programmers than computer architectures.

After our star expert left the company, I was the company authority, the one people called if they had a complex question about the architecture or optimization techniques for our high-performance computers. Before the other expert left, he and I had co-developed a vectorized mathematical library containing various numerical analysis algorithms—including eigenvalue solvers and Fast Fourier Transforms (FFTs)—that was included with each vectorizing FORTRAN compiler delivered with new versions of the supercomputer operating systems. Perhaps this description is too technical for many readers, but it sounds good...and gives an idea of how specialized my work was.

I also wrote complex FFT computer code to run optimally on a new IBM architecture, which led to a multimillion-dollar computer sale in South Africa. The account sales representative made a lot of money and sent me a dozen pink baby roses. My boss refused to even give me a $50 dinner-for-two award, reasoning that we shouldn't be doing business in South Africa, anyway. I wasn't buying that, but never knew his real motives.

By 1987, headhunters were calling me weekly. I'd turned down several job offers from our supercomputer competitors and customers (oil companies, universities, US government agencies, etc.) because I wanted to be loyal to my company. But the company didn't share that sentiment toward me when their subsidiary supercomputer company, where I was on loan, abruptly went out of business on April 17, 1989. When the company dissolved, about 3,100 employees at the subsidiary lost their jobs.

I could have taken another position at the parent company, but since I'd had multiple psychotic episodes during my ten-year tenure, this was probably a good excuse to get rid of me (though a senior sales rep once told me I was still more productive than the other analysts during those times after a psychotic break). I would have needed to work only two more months to be vested in the company's retirement plan. I do understand that long-term disability and retirement pay can be expensive. My boss had to consider the company's bottom line.

After Steve and I divorced in 1990, I didn't have a permanent job, a home, or child support. Steve's mother owned the house we were living in, so I purchased the first house the realtor showed me. I needed a suitable

16

home for the children to live before the judge made the custody evaluation. But the judge recused himself for a trumped-up reason, so Steve and I settled out of court on the joint custody arrangements. It was preposterous. Because of my bipolar disorder, Steve wanted to see the children every day to make sure I didn't harm them. I could only drive our children a distance of fifty miles to see my mother every other weekend. If we went on vacation, I had to take another adult with us who was well-acquainted with the symptoms of mania and psychosis.

I became self-employed and consulted with a diverse customer base for a wide range of high-performance computers, including the company which had ousted me, a Japanese supercomputer company, the nearby state university, a new parallel architecture computer manufacturer, and an engineering company. I converted computer programs for scientific applications to run on almost every high-performance computer architecture available. One computational fluid dynamics code pinpointed locations to drill in the Gulf of Mexico oil basins. I presented papers about my results at two national geosciences conferences. I also optimized computer codes for Army battle management modeling, among other applications.

For eight years during the 90s, I also worked part time as a research scientist at a US national laboratory. For a short time there, I was manager of the High-Performance Computing Center User Services, but I couldn't take the harassment from my boss. He scolded me for doing algorithm consulting with the scientists. Instead, he wanted me to organize the conferences and support the attendees as an administrative assistant would do.

During a national holiday, before one of my paper presentations, I needed to test my computer code, but my boss wanted me to work during his conference. I asked what he needed me to do. His response was "make copies, get coffee, or anything else that is needed." I protested. He slammed the door so hard that some of the pictures fell off the wall. But he finally agreed to have an administrative assistant do it. My stint in that role didn't last much longer.

Biotech Company Meets Bipolar Disorder

In 1994, my gynecologist persuaded me to have a prophylactic hysterectomy with both ovaries removed to try to help with my mood swings. I was only forty-three years old. I'm neither convinced of the efficacy of the procedure in regulating my moods, nor understand the effects of hormone replacement therapy on my bipolar disorder.

Earlier that year, I had licensed computer software from a US national laboratory that searched for genes and elucidated features in DNA sequences, then founded a biotech company that further developed and marketed this software to pharmaceutical and biotech companies internationally. At first, I distributed the working deliverable software package I was given, but later, when the source code was delivered to me, some of it was missing. This included the code to access and use GenBank, the National Institutes of Health (NIH) genetic sequence database, in the analyses. The interface to access the software itself was even missing, leaving broken links to the code's functionality.

I took exception, but the scientist who'd developed the software and the tech transfer licensing officer maintained that I had received all that I'd paid for. I complained to the lab director, who upheld their claims. I was later told by someone working in his office that he'd said, "She's just a bitch out to make trouble."

Before we exhibited at a human genome international conference in 1996, one of my employees, Brian, analyzed the broken software and added a Java user interface. Java was a new, cutting-edge programming language that was first formally released in 1995, but none of our competitors had a Java interface at that time.

For a subsequent conference, Brian was running out of time when upgrading to the latest Java version. It was not upward compatible. The constructs and syntax were significantly different. I found it amusing that my employee enlisted assistance from the CEO—me—to help him finish the conversion in time. A few years ago, I found Brian on LinkedIn. He was vice-president for software development at the company that created the Java programming language.

In 1997, I assumed a technical role at my own company again when I borrowed a multiprocessor workstation to demonstrate the use of four processors in parallel using some of our software. The code was written in C, an object-oriented programming language to which I'd had no exposure. I only knew the FORTRAN language, which was an ancient relic at that point. It was a couple of days before an international conference, and the consultant I'd lined up to do the conversion had to cancel.

So Megan (age thirteen) and I went to my office and stayed up all night to see if I could do it myself. She fell asleep on my couch. At 5:30 a.m., I woke her up screaming, "It works!" She got excited too. The only business open at that time was a gas station/convenience store. We each bought a soda and a Moon Pie, and we drove around the town a-hootin' and a-hollerin'!

My company developed seven new gene-finding products, and I wrote and negotiated numerous contracts with customers, strategic partners, and distributors, including copyright, co-marketing, beta testing, and end-user license agreements. We exhibited at eight trade shows and advertised in leading trade journals. In addition to our business board of directors, I assembled a Technical Advisory Board made up of nine leading experts from the US and Europe. The company was funded by $850K in Small Business Innovation and Research (SBIR) Phase I and II grants from the Department of Energy (DOE).

In 1995, in the midst of these years of business success, I experienced another psychotic episode. I gave my van to a neighbor down the street (who later returned it) and a few prized possessions to children who had walked past my house, but I did not harm anyone. A male business associate had convinced me to cut back on my lithium dosage before a human genome conference, where my company would be exhibiting, because he believed I would sell more software if I were a little manic. This was the only time, before my psychotic episode in 2018, that I'd modified my psychotropic drug regimen without a doctor's supervision.

On a Sunday, while neighbors were leaving for church services, several police cars showed up in front of my house. They broke into my home and found me in my bedroom reading my dad's Bible. When I resisted giving it up, they handcuffed my hands behind my back, bound my legs with tape, and picked me up. One began beating me on my back with a billystick, but they dropped me on the floor when I said, "I'm *not* Rodney King!"

Assessing that I was too berserk to mesh with their current patient population, the local state mental institution refused to take me, so the police took me to a small, little-known private hospital, where I was locked in a cage with only a metal frame cot without bedding. Later, I asked a nurse to check my back for bruises. She said there were many, but refused to believe my story about the police, saying, "Now Honey, you know it was a friend or family member that beat you like that!"

I didn't report the incident to the authorities because one of the last things a business owner wants is negative press on the front page of a newspaper! Though I never learned who sent the police to my house, I was too embarrassed to live in my neighborhood, so my children and I moved into an apartment across town for a few months. I paid both rent and a mortgage.

The small, private hospital had released me too soon. Within a couple of weeks, my psychosis returned, and I was admitted to a local hospital with a psychiatric wing. The psychiatrist who treated me there took me off lithium and replaced it with a variety of medication cocktails over the next five years.

These treatments included some combination of mood stabilizers, antipsychotics, anticonvulsants, and antidepressants. I felt as though the concoctions were hit-and-miss choices, thrown at a dart board just to see what sticks (works). Some drugs made me manic. The antidepressant Wellbutrin comes to mind. Other medicines made me appear to be a zombie with what's called a *flat affect*. I took drugs from all classes—including

19

Depakote, Haldol, Risperdal, Tegretol, Geodon, and others—too many to remember.

Due to my pre-existing conditions and job situations, I didn't have health insurance or prescription drug coverage during most years between 1990 and 2003 (when I qualified for Medicare, but even then, I would hit the coverage gap by April). Geodon alone cost $980 out-of-pocket each month. When my income stopped in 2000, I begged my psychiatrist to put me back on lithium. It was cheap! He refused, so I changed to a psychiatrist who would. The tremors and other side effects resumed, but I couldn't afford the other medications. At some point, I also began taking the mood stabilizer lamotrigine (Lamictal).

In 1996, the founder and CEO of Oxford Molecular and his chief technical officer (CTO) met with me at my office to discuss buying my company. Headquartered in the UK, Oxford Molecular was the largest biotech software company in the world at the time. We agreed to wait until the DOE contracts were completed.

In 1998, I was an invited speaker at a gene-finding algorithm development international conference at Cold Spring Harbor Laboratory. Nobel Laureate Dr. James Watson, co-discoverer of the double-helix structure of DNA, lived in Cold Spring Harbor, New York, but didn't attend any of the sessions. He only came over once to have dessert with a researcher from Russia whose father was a friend and fellow Nobel Laureate—and with me. Watson was on the Board of Directors for Oxford Molecular and wanted to discuss them buying my company.

I was extremely manic at the time, but I was able to "keep it together" for thirty minutes or so. I don't know if Watson could tell. Their letter came to set up a meeting during another period of severe mania, just short of psychosis. My company was being run at that time by a member of our board of directors. Somehow, the letter was lost without me ever seeing it. Later that year, during another period of extreme mania, I sold my company for a fraction of what I thought it was worth.

Debilitating Disability

There's nothing more debilitating about a disability than the
way people treat you over it.

—Solange Nicole, Author/Poet

Diversity Director

After I sold my company, my close friend Mark offered me a job as a diversity director for a university/national laboratory consortium. This didn't require my technical or business expertise. I established the Research Alliance for Minorities (RAM) Program and recruited minority students, mostly from Historically Black Colleges and Universities (HBCUs). I paired them with scientists at the national laboratory for summer research projects. I also selected community leaders for personal mentoring.

Though I rented apartments for the students near the laboratory, many of them preferred to sleep on the floor at my house and commute thirty miles each way to the lab. The students were demoralized by experiences like the time they got into the swimming pool at their apartment complex, and all the Caucasians got out. This was 1999!

The students became close friends with my children, sometimes accompanying us on short vacation trips.

One student in particular stood out. I'll call her Amanda for this story, to protect her privacy. Her mother was a heroin addict when she was born, so she was raised by her grandmother. For her summer research project, she did an independent study of the techniques used by Sir Ian Wilmut and his research team in 1996 at the University of Edinburgh to clone the first mammal, a lamb named Dolly, from an adult sheep somatic cell (a somatic cell is any cell that is neither an egg nor a sperm). Dolly was cloned from a mammary gland cell, hence her name.

A year after Amanda's summer internship, her grandmother died, right before she graduated from an HBCU with a BS in mathematics. She had no place to go, so she lived with me for six months.

Inspired by her successful research project, she told me she wanted to get a master's degree in Nuclear Radiology. I'd never heard of such a degree, but I didn't discourage her, just like I hadn't when she wanted to research cloning. I had thought that would be too hard for an undergraduate. I still don't understand it!

I researched and found that the nearby state university offered a Medical Physics master's degree on the path towards a PhD in Nuclear Engineering. I knew a couple of nuclear engineers. They were brilliant. I knew the degree would be tough, but I still encouraged her, despite my doubts. I called the head of the Nuclear Engineering Department personally and set up an appointment for us to meet with him. Like me, he didn't discourage her. He signed her up for the fall semester, and she did quite well in some courses that would have been tough for me.

Unfortunately, her time living with me was cut short, because my mental health was in decline. I seemed to be cycling between hypomania and mild depression in an episode with mixed features (mixed state). Her sister, who lived 1,000 miles away in Texas, came to get her. She probably would've completed the work for a master's, at least, had she not had to leave and move in with her sister.

Years later, she stayed with me for a couple of nights during a business trip to train some area high school math teachers to use the curriculum developed by a major textbook publisher. I lamented that I'd been disabled since 2000 and hadn't achieved or contributed much to society.

She said, "That's not true. In every presentation I make, I tell my teachers about how you encouraged me to achieve all I could do—to persevere to reach my goals. I challenge them to motivate their students to do the same. So, your legacy has helped so many people during the years you were disabled."

She's currently a regional vice-president of Professional Learning for a major publishing company.

I lost my job as diversity director in 2000. I quit, and they didn't renew my contract. No way to know which happened first. Doesn't matter. The cause was the same either way—my mental illness.

Hoodwinked by My Cofounder

In spite of my poor mental health, a talented MBA student and I formed a genomics company to investigate proteomes in 2000. A proteome is the entire set of proteins made by an organism.

I wrote five SBIR proposals, one each for detection of influenza, streptococcus, anthrax, Lyme's disease, and gonorrhea. We were awarded $100K by the National Science Foundation (NSF) for our influenza project proposal. I was the Principal Investigator (PI).

Before the award was announced, I began experiencing a mixed state, and the cofounder voted me out of the company. I had unknowingly signed incorporation documents that gave him 52 percent of the company.

Since I was the PI on the influenza project, the NSF offered me the grant, but I was too sick to form another company to do the research and development. So, I gave the grant to my cofounder. With that seed money, he has become a very successful entrepreneur, new business development consultant, and venture capitalist.

I was devastated. I felt betrayed. I'd spent so much time teaching him about small business, in general, and specifically, the SBIR process. These were things you don't learn in a formal MBA academic setting. I'm still resentful, wondering how my professional life might have turned out had I not had this debilitating disease. I have to agree with my former father-in-law: "Partnership is the worst damn ship I ever rode!"

Life With Alan

I met Alan through AOL Instant Messenger (AIM). I messaged him because I was curious about his screen name (themagicbox). Also, I was lonely and always looking for someone interesting to connect with. He told me *The Magic Box* was a 1951 film starring his favorite actor, Robert Donat. That intrigued me, so we began messaging and finally met. We lived about one hundred miles apart.

I was officially declared disabled by the Social Security Administration in 2003. That year, Alan came to live with and take care of me, primarily to monitor my mental health. He also did all the cooking, housecleaning, and bookkeeping—he even gave me insulin shots for my diabetes.

Alan has Bachelor of Arts degrees in History and English. He taught me a lot about history, especially about politics and former presidents. His favorite president was James K. Polk. Alan kept the TV tuned to Fox News all day, and we enjoyed many discussions about politics, especially during presidential election cycles. Alan also had a knack for remembering dates. He would often greet me in the morning with facts like, "Charles J. Guiteau assassinated President James Garfield 130 years ago today," or "Today's September 17, 2009. It would have been Hank Williams' eighty-sixth birthday."

Alan was also a movie buff. He had an extensive collection of movie DVDs, including many classics. His number one favorite movie of all time was the 1953 film *Shane*, starring Alan Ladd. We watched at least one movie each day. We also shared a love of music. He had many CDs—old-time favorites, like the Carter Family, Johnny Cash, Hank Williams Sr., and The Louvin Brothers; more modern artists, such as Kris Kristofferson, Willie Nelson, Waylon Jennings, and Merle Haggard; and many old-timey folk musicians, like Doc Watson, Woody Guthrie, Cisco Houston, and Kelly Harrell.

Alan had been a talented artist (painting, drawing, photography, and other art forms) in the past, but he had long since given them up. He didn't like my art choices, so he replaced many of the paintings and wall hangings throughout my house with an eclectic assortment of framed pictures—some with autographs, lobby cards, and movie posters. His art featured Robert Donat, and included Hank Williams Sr., Eddie Cantor, Marie Dressler, Jean Harlow, and even Dwight Eisenhower, to name a few. My favorite of his movie posters was *The Inn of the Sixth Happiness* with Ingrid Bergman, Curt Jürgens, and Robert Donat.

Secretly, I was somewhat annoyed by his taking charge of my home—changing the decor, controlling the TV, and commandeering some of the rooms, but I didn't complain. This was in part because I usually defer power to anyone, especially a man, who is assertive, and probably more importantly, I felt obligated to give in because he did me such a great favor to give up his current style of living to move to Knoxville to take care of me.

I was uncomfortable with my older, conservative friends knowing I was *living in sin* with a man. One of my neighbors confronted me about that one day, and I assured her that the relationship was purely platonic, though I doubt if she knew what that meant. One morning, completely out of the blue, Betty, my closest friend from church and twenty years my senior, showed up to visit. Alan came to my bedroom to get me and I panicked. I immediately addressed the elephant in the room, assuring Betty that our relationship was nonsexual. She blew me away with her reply, "Can't you put something in his coffee?"

Alan lived with me until 2013, after my health had drastically improved and his health had drastically declined. He was in constant back, hip, and neck pain, and he frequently fell. He would pass out for a few seconds, but he would quickly bounce back. Unlike a cat, he had many more than nine lives. Once he fell in the shower, knocking a large hole in the tile. When I found him, his head was completely through the hole, looking upward between the walls.

It became clear to me that we couldn't continue our living arrangement. He jokingly says I kicked him out on his birthday, September 26. That's the day his brother Sam took him to Virginia to live near five of his six siblings. Now, nearly ten years after he left, we are still very close, and we talk by phone almost every day, ending each conversation with "love ya!"

A Career Cut Short

Excessive medications and subsequent obesity—at one point, I got up to 200 pounds—led to other issues such as diabetes and heart disease which, when combined with worsening mental illness, kept me disabled after 2000.

Ironically, lithium, the original treatment I was prescribed, caused side effects that led to my becoming disabled. When I first began taking lithium in the early 1980s, my blood levels were checked weekly because the therapeutic dose and the lethal dose were close together. Sometimes they were high, so I had some of the lithium toxicity (poisoning) symptoms: nausea, vomiting, diarrhea, severe hand tremors, impaired balance, ataxia (poor muscle control), confusion, and changes in vision. Occasionally, I could barely walk due to muscle weakness or spasms and balance issues.

My long-term essential tremor was the most noticeable and debilitating of my lithium side effects. By the time I was in my forties, others would sometimes have to feed me at a restaurant. I could barely use a fork or spoon. I would miss my mouth, often jabbing my face or dropping food in my lap or on the floor. I wouldn't drink coffee or any other liquid in front of others, even from a toddler's sippy cup, because my hands shook so uncontrollably the liquid would splash out all over the place.

These symptoms improved considerably after I quit taking lithium again in 2012, but I'm still embarrassed to eat in public. I have a familial resting tremor and symptoms of drug-induced parkinsonism, which appear to be permanent. I was given the antipsychotic quetiapine (Seroquel) to replace lithium in 2012. In 2024, a new skin biopsy test (SYN-One) provided pathological evidence of Parkinson's disease.

I was not permitted to have even a part-time job after 2003, because of Social Security Disability Income (SSDI) rules. Since SSDI was my primary source of income, I couldn't afford to lose it. I was never well enough to try to hold a full-time job again after that. I did help some friends without receiving payment when I was well enough to do so. Since I actually became disabled after 2000, professionally speaking, I basically slept like Rip Van Winkle for the next two decades!

In 2007, Mark (the friend who'd offered me the Diversity Director job) and another friend, Emily, opened an investment account with TD Ameritrade. He said he didn't want my brain to atrophy and got me involved. Mark and Emily funded the account. All I could provide was sweat equity. I used numerical modeling and other means for studying stock technicals and fundamentals to make options and stock trading selections. I'm still a part of this venture, though I haven't made any trades since 2011—the year I broke my hip due to leg spasms, another lithium side effect.

Finding the "Want To"

In January 2012, my memory and cognitive skills had gotten so poor that it took me a month to solve a simple high-school-level math problem. Later that year, upon my psychiatrist's recommendation, I was admitted into a comprehensive, long-term care facility. It was presumed that this would be my permanent residence.

But God had a different plan for my life. I remembered a sermon I'd heard years before by Rev. Allan C. Oggs Sr.—"You Gotta Have the Want To." At birth, he was diagnosed with severe cerebral palsy and was never expected to walk, talk, or see. He said that as a child he fell frequently, "But You Gotta Get Up Again!" By the grace of God, he had a family and became a Protestant minister who preached all over the United States for over fifty years.

My first grandchild gave me **my** "want to." She was over a year old, and I'd never been able to stand up and hold her due to my risk for falls.

I observed that the long-term care facility's administrative staff didn't work on Sundays and the nurses usually stayed in the skilled nursing wing, so one Saturday night near the end of 2012, I called my transportation service and *broke out* early the next morning! The driver took me back home to resume living with my roommate, Alan.

After I escaped, as I like to say, I changed my primary care physician (PCP) to be the family medicine doctor who'd pinpointed lithium as the major cause of my balance and leg spasm issues during my hospital admission earlier in 2012. I'd fallen three times in the hospital rehab gym, and the nurses insisted on having me admitted after my third fall. I'd been taking so many medications (twenty-seven, according to Elijah) that each time I saw him, my PCP felt like a failure if he couldn't take me off at least two or three more of them. My health dramatically improved.

I also convinced him to monitor and manage my bipolar disorder with only the mood stabilizer, lamotrigine, and to take me off the antipsychotic, quetiapine, because I was exhibiting mild, potentially irreversible signs of tardive dyskinesia (TDK), including involuntary facial movements, uncontrollable side-to-side rubbing of the backs of my teeth with my tongue, and making sucking motions and sounds with my mouth.

During a visit to my PCP in September 2013, I told him I'd made a mobile app for my granddaughter Sara's second birthday. Looking shocked, he wrote in my chart, "and her brain is back!" Starting in the early 90s, when I was uninsurable due to preexisting conditions, my out-of-pocket prescription drug costs had averaged over $2,000 a month, but they dropped to less than $600 for the entire year in 2013.

I was elated that most of my health issues were under control, but I often remarked, "This bipolar disorder isn't going anywhere unless there's a major medical breakthrough." I still had periods of manic symptoms, including talking nonstop, euphoria, racing thoughts, difficulty focusing, poor judgment, and overactivity, interspersed occasionally with depression.

Despite my doubt and unbelief, in February 2016, a church pastor volunteered to pray for me, telling me God had neither caused nor wanted me to be mentally ill. He asked me to never say "I am mentally ill" again.

Both Megan, a pharmacist, and Elijah, an emergency medicine physician, chose careers in healthcare, but formal training couldn't replace the experiential learning they gained about bipolar disorder by growing up in my household. Megan could tell right away that I was different—just by talking with me by phone. I listened without talking incessantly, and I could focus. In April 2016, I visited Elijah and his family in Chicago. When I arrived, I asked if he could tell my mental health had improved considerably.

He said, "Mom, I've known you to have a mental illness for over thirty years. You haven't been here an hour, and you expect me to say you don't?"

Before that visit, I wasn't able to keep my two granddaughters, Sara and Madison, alone for more than four hours due to my mental illness. The first night of the visit, Elijah and his wife, Nicole, left me alone with their four-year-old, their two-year-old, and their four-month-old while they went only five minutes away. I was baby Ethan's first sitter. By that weekend I was caring for all three of my grandchildren by myself for over twelve hours while Elijah and Nicole went to downtown Chicago, an hour and a half away. If anyone doubts my breakthrough, that's the only proof they need.

None of my family or friends disputed that I was better than I had been. I wasn't talking 90 mph or interrupting them all the time. But some people didn't credit supernatural healing by a higher power, suggesting it was just the result of psychotherapy and an improved lifestyle—diet, exercise, sleep, etc.

I became defensive, even somewhat angry, if anyone suggested I was paranoid, or getting a little manicky, especially if they'd asked if I was taking my medications.

Whenever I would have any doubts about my healing, I would recite in my head my Christian mantra: "For God has not given us a spirit of fear; but of power, and of love and of a sound mind" (2 Timothy 1:7 New King James Version® [NKJV]).

Life was going well for a while, and I felt healed. So, I was caught off guard when, a couple of years later, I had a major psychotic episode.

In the remaining chapters of this book, I will give an in-depth account of the gradual escalation of events in 2017–2018 (paranoia, rejection, elevated mood, extreme happiness, extravagant spending, overestimation of my abilities, and impulsive behavior) leading up to, through, and following the 2018 psychotic episode.

PART II

DISASTER IN THE MAKING

Meemaw1 and Meemaw2

August 2017–May 2018

Meemaw2

May 23–27, 2018

PART II

DISASTER IN THE MAKING

Meghan Page Morrell?

August 2017–May 2018

Montana

March 23–27, 2018

Danger, Will Robinson! Danger!

Have you seen our robot?

—Will Robinson, *Lost in Space*

Meet Hilda

I was a young teenager when the sci-fi TV series *Lost in Space* aired on CBS 1965–1968, inspired by the 1812 novel *The Swiss Family Robinson* and the comic book *Space Family Robinson*. Each week I looked forward to the next adventure for Will, his older sisters Penny and Judy, and their parents, Professor John and Dr. Maureen Robinson. Dr. Zachary Smith was the villain, an agent of an unnamed, evil foreign government, who constantly tried to sabotage the mission.

My favorite character (besides Will) was the Robot Model B-9, which had no name and was usually just referred to as Robot. Robot was Will's constant companion and was programmed to warn him of any impending danger, including Dr. Smith's malevolent mischief. I still recall the robot's cold, emotionless, automaton voice: "Warning! Warning! or Danger! Danger, Will Robinson!" or the often quoted "That does not compute!"

My fascination with Robot is not surprising, given my interests in computers, mathematics, and science. When I was young (well before the days of cellphones), I dreamed about having a device connected to my rotary-dial landline phone that would allow me to see the person I was talking to. What was science fiction has now become reality.

Now my dream is a wristband-wearable robot, which I call Hilda, named in honor of my favorite dog. The original Hilda was a Doberman Pinscher who died in 1973 from a heat stroke, while whelping the only pup in her first litter. My robot Hilda could seamlessly integrate with smartphone apps and body sensors, using advanced data analysis and machine learning (ML) algorithms to monitor and manage my bipolar disorder by analyzing and predicting my mood and behaviors. Hilda could alert family, friends, mental health professionals, and even me to warning signs, indicating that I might be heading into the dangerous territory of moderate mania. Maybe she could even contact a law enforcement officer if I'd already plunged full steam into a psychotic manic episode with no family or friends nearby.

In particular, Hilda could be trained specifically to recognize some of my manic symptoms: irregular sleep patterns, incessant and rapid speech bouncing from topic to topic, boundless energy, increased activity levels, relationship conflicts, overcommitment to too many projects that are not completed, distraction, radical mood swings from feeling unusually happy and upbeat to sad, irritable, or angry, and, for me, even something so bizarre as excessive stress sweat odors from my apocrine glands.

You might think this design is farfetched, but you probably already use many of the artificial intelligence (AI) technologies that would make Hilda possible. If you use Google or Apple Maps, you are using machine learning (ML), a type of AI. Word processors and texting apps use ML, deep learning, and natural language processing to identify mistakes and suggest or make corrections (many times incorrect, and sometimes even embarrassing). Alexa, Google Assistant, and Apple's Siri use AI, ML, and automation technologies. Scientists are even using ML in human olfactory research. These and many other applications we use every day could be used to design Hilda. Biorobotics like this for use with many diseases, including bipolar disorder and other mental illnesses, is a hot topic for research right now.

Some features of Hilda have already been implemented in other health monitoring applications. But there are many barriers to completing my dream robot—concerns about data privacy, miniaturization, cost, storage, data processing speed, algorithm development and verification, pilot program testing, poor usability, and lack of patient early adopters.

Anosognosia

Sometimes I intentionally hid (or tried to hide) symptoms that some people would have recognized as danger signals. On those rare occasions when family or friends *did* suggest to me that something might be wrong, I would protest or downplay it, sometimes getting defensive or even angry. I didn't want to recognize or admit to any problems. Many times, when I felt an issue might be cropping up, I would squash the thought—the *ostrich effect* (though I know ostriches don't really bury their heads in the sand). If I couldn't see it, it wasn't there.

There's a fancy name for this reaction—*anosognosia*…an inability to recognize a disorder or illness that is clinically evident. The National Alliance on Mental Illness (NAMI) describes anosognosia as:

> When someone rejects a diagnosis of mental illness, it's tempting to say that they're "in denial." But someone with acute mental illness may not be thinking clearly enough to consciously choose denial. They may instead be experiencing "lack of insight" or "lack of awareness." The formal medical term for this medical condition is anosognosia, from the Greek meaning "to not know a disease."
> —National Alliance on Mental Illness

(https://www.nami.org/About-Mental-Illness/Common-with-Mental-Illness/Anosognosia)

My anosognosia began long before my first psychotic episode in late 1982, after which I was obliged to admit that I had a mental illness. Any time my emotional state was compared to my father's, I strongly protested. I'd never seen any of his negative emotions, only love and kindness, though I'd been told he'd had a few psychotic episodes. People always told me that he had lots of friends and that "everybody liked him." I assumed he'd gotten sick because he was so kind and easily taken advantage of.

Once, during the time of my first divorce in 1981, I missed a lunch meeting with a friend because I'd forgotten about it. I was too active—with my mood elevated and my thoughts racing. I had too much trouble concentrating to remember appointments and other obligations. My friend was seeing a psychiatrist and recommended I see him too.

When the psychiatrist discovered that my father had had mental issues, he told me he wanted to admit me to a hospital and regulate the dosage of some medications he thought would help me. But "admit me to a [mental] hospital" were fighting words for me! I stood up and quietly left the room, never to come back. I understand now that this is common behavior with anosognosia.

There were many danger signals in 2017 and 2018 leading up to my severe episode, but they were visible only to a few isolated people, most of whom knew nothing or little about bipolar disorder. Usually, they only saw a small piece of the puzzle and weren't alarmed enough to communicate with my family, friends, or professionals. Hilda would have had all the information. She could have analyzed the data and alerted a list of contacts that some intervention was needed in time to circumvent my eventual psychotic breakdown in 2018.

Facebook Romance Scam

When I consider Life, 'tis all a cheat;
Yet, fooled with hope, men favour the deceit;
Trust on, and think to-morrow will repay:
To-morrow's falser than the former day;
Lies worse; and while it says, we shall be blest
With some new joys, cuts off what we possesst.

—John Dryden, *Aureng-Zebe*

Caught by a Catfish

In 1990, my ex-husband Steve had said, "If'n I ever get rid of thissun, I ain't never gettin me nary a nuthern!"

My sentiments exactly. Sometime within the past ten years, I relaxed the condition to: "If He wants me to marry again, God will have to bring a man to my front door and show me a sign that he's THE ONE."

On August 21, 2017, I observed the Great American Eclipse with one hundred percent visibility. It was eerie and exhilarating at the same time. It gradually became darker and quieter. The birds stopped singing. They must have thought it was bedtime. Then it happened! The moon totally blocked out the sun. All I could see was its corona. It was as if the Creator God of the Universe had simultaneously revealed His omnipotence, omniscience, and omnipresence fully to me in this awesome cosmic event. And it was on the 21st of the month—my favorite number!

So, it's not surprising that I interpreted the message I found in my Facebook Messenger app that night from a stranger named Bill Moore to be from THE ONE. His profile portrayed a deeply religious Christian man with a deep-seated love for and devotion to his daughter. Though this was not important to me, he was also pictured with an expensive sports car. Maybe a Ferrari? So, I answered his text.

Our hour-long exchange of messages three days later confirmed that he was the perfect man for me.

Still reeling with excitement, that night I shared the news about my new potential relationship with two of my millennial friends, Nancy and Wesley. Each is internet-savvy, but both lack my senior wisdom and naivete. Wesley immediately texted back that the guy was probably a catfish. He had to explain to me that a catfish is someone who creates a fake online profile to attract victims for a romance scam. This scheme is perpetrated against both women and men from all educational, professional, and socioeconomic backgrounds.

34

Nancy was suspicious as well. She told me how to use Google's *Search with Image* capability to try to find the person whose images he might have stolen to set up his Facebook profile. To my surprise, I found a guy on Myspace, an older social media platform, who had some of the same photos. His name was Jeff Jennings, and he liked to crochet and make quilts. It was easy for me to believe Jeff was the fake one. After all, REAL men don't eat quiche, crochet, or make quilts! And the pictures of Bill were so sexy.

Had I thought it through, however, I would have realized that it was far more likely that the catfish would be using the modern platform Facebook and had stolen the photos from Myspace, which was a relic.

When I spoke with Bill the next morning, I shared all this information. He pretended to be unaware of the term "catfish" and appeared to be hurt that I would question him like that. He insisted that he was authentic, and the other guy had stolen his identity. I obviously wanted to believe him, so I continued on with the charade. I'd already taken the bait and was hooked!

Meemaw, You Are So Gullible

Bill was slick! I was gullible, lonely, and desperate—a perfect victim for a romance scam.

Our *relationship* was accelerated—exactly the norm of two weeks for a scam like this. Scammers can't afford to spend a lot of time on a victim who won't pay them money. It squanders time from baiting victims who will pay anywhere from five thousand to hundreds of thousands of dollars, in some cases. Since they're trying to scam multiple people simultaneously, they quickly switch to a pet name to keep from making mistakes. Mine was "Honey."

Bill's story was a romance scam classic. According to him, his company provided the project management for a subcontractor to Schlumberger on an oil drilling job off the coast of the UK. Near the end of our two-week courtship, he asked for money. He claimed that the project was finishing up, but because of cost overruns, he had exceeded his budget. Schlumberger had approved a revised payment amount, but the extra money wouldn't arrive for two weeks. His workers were independent contractors to his own private company, and they needed to be paid. If I would send him $6,000 by Western Union, he would pay me back in two weeks when he visited me after returning stateside.

I'd been cautiously optimistic from the beginning, often telling Elijah that Bill was too good to be true. Elijah would say, "Then he probably *is*!" I had ignored many red flags since the obvious warnings from Nancy and Wesley, because I secretly enjoyed the romancing that I'd missed for the past twenty-five years. But when Bill asked for money, I knew! I googled "oil rig scam" and found the *HuffPost* article "How A Billion-Dollar Internet Scam Is Breaking Hearts and Bank Accounts" by Ann Brenoff (July 2017).

The next time he called, I dropped him like a hot potato. I told him I wasn't looking for a relationship when he came into my life, and I wouldn't miss him when he was gone! That was borne out by my family. A few weeks later, I told Nicole about the scam and asked if she'd noticed anything different in my mood or countenance. She had no idea the whirlwind romance was over.

In previous years, the short, two-week cyber romance scam would have sent me into a manic tailspin. Each of my two relationships between 2014 and 2015 had made me hypomanic. But when the 2017 scam was exposed, I was actually relieved that he was a fake. Deep down, I knew he was too good to be true!

Though I don't necessarily believe it was connected to the cyberattacks I experienced in the fall of 2017, the Facebook romance scam certainly laid the foundation for the paranoia I experienced once the actual cyberattacks began. If nothing else, it highlighted just how unsafe the internet can be—even for an information technology specialist.

Cyber Insecurity

For we are not fighting against flesh-and-blood enemies, but against evil rulers and authorities of the unseen world, against mighty powers in this dark world, and against evil spirits in the heavenly places.

—Eph. 6:12 (NLT)

Cyberwarfare

Information technology (IT) has been one of my passions for over fifty years. My computer exposure began as an undergraduate in the 1970s. In my senior year, I taught a sophomore-level computer science lab using the FORTRAN programming language to solve numerical analysis problems. My mathematics PhD dissertation was a blend of algebraic number theory and computing. My first job after graduation was with the second-largest computer company in the US at the time (behind IBM). In 1993, I founded a bioinformatics company that sold computer software to find genes in DNA sequences.

Despite my computer technology background, I wasn't prepared for the onslaught of cyberattacks I experienced in the latter half of 2017 and early 2018. I believe this blitzkrieg was one of the major factors that contributed to my 2018 psychotic episode. These events increased my paranoia and made me question reality. In retrospect, my response to the attacks also offered some early warning signs of my impending psychosis—but without a Hilda to put the pieces together, the full picture wasn't clear to me or those around me.

When I insisted in 2017 that I was fighting cyberwarfare with an international crime ring, you can imagine the skepticism and ridicule I received from my family and friends. Elijah maintained that all of these cyber infractions were not perpetrated by a single group "out to get me." He said some of the instances individually might be cybercrimes, but there was not a group of people reacting to each of my attempts to discover and correct what they were doing.

I wasn't convinced! Though much of what I experienced might have logical explanations, some are worth mentioning, because they contributed to my paranoia and cyber insecurity.

Phone Clones

There were several indications that one or more of my cellphones had been cloned. One indicator was that my communications were hacked. SIM cards were copied to exact duplicates of my phones—manufacturer, model, operating system, etc. Cellphone messages were intercepted, and I stopped getting texts in a timely manner. On October 8, 2017, I discovered that each of my active cellphones had clones off the coast of Nigeria. I used the Google utility "find my device" and made screen copies of the maps showing the location of my devices, including both those in my house and the replicas in Africa. When I found the clones, an obnoxious, high-pitched tone sounded on my LG V10 phone for five minutes, and then my phone was locked, and the PIN I'd set to make emergency calls was changed.

I drove to a local AT&T store and was told the phone couldn't be fixed. It was about a year old and had cost $850. The sales associate sold me a new $500 Samsung J7 with 16 GB internal memory, and incorrectly told me I would not be able to transfer my photos from my previous phone's 32 GB microSD card with 32 GB of storage to the new phone, which had less internal memory (which is not the same as storage). He led me to believe I had lost all my photos. Later, Elijah told me all I'd needed to do to fix my original LG V10 was to remove the battery and then put it back in—and, in addition, the microSD card was interchangeable between the two phones. But the sales associate wouldn't have collected a big commission if he'd told me that!

I had more cyberattacks on the J7. A sales support specialist at AT&T told me it was because the hackers could intercept my messages from a cell tower, since they knew my phone number and SIM card password. Since many people had my cell number, I didn't want to change it.

So I purchased another phone using Megan's address and an out-of-state phone number. Didn't help. That one was hacked within fifteen minutes by a bogus text with a vicious link when I tried to update an app. Several tech support people had told me that the microphones and cameras on my devices could be turned on remotely. So I concluded they'd gotten my new phone number either when the sales associate called my new number from my old phone, or that they'd heard him tell me the number out loud.

Whenever I had problems with the phone I was using, I would often move the SIM card to one of the others to make it an operable cellphone. Then I would do a complete factory reset of the former phone, usually not taking the time to move pictures to a microSD card or back up my messages. I lost a lot of information. I bought so many phones during this fiasco in 2017 that Elijah once called and asked which of my "drug dealer phones" I was using!

Cyberphobia

My favorite response from one of my requests for help came from an older technical support team member at an electronics retailer. And when I say *favorite*, I mean most horrific. He told me a lot of what I was seeing could be dangerous or even fatal. He said I was being targeted and asked if I knew someone who was out to get me or wanted me dead. Maybe an ex? Was I a public figure? Did I drive a later model car with a computer? Did I own a microwave or smart TV? He suggested I sell my house and car and move to a remote place with only a landline and older model car and TV. He said my cellphone could trigger an explosion of other electronic devices and urged me to leave the store as soon as I could. I asked if it would be okay to use the restroom first. He said he wouldn't recommend it. Maybe he was more of a lunatic than I was! He didn't seem the type who would be pulling my leg for amusement.

I became paranoid. I was too terrified to drive—afraid my car would blow up. After all, the Crime Ring was listening through the microphones on my devices.

After leaving the electronics store, I drove to meet my friends Dan and Karen at a Chick-fil-A next door to a bank. I parked on the far side of the bank and left all my electronic equipment inside my car. I even returned with a tablet when I discovered it was in a bag I had carried inside. I told my friends about my experience at the electronics store, and they convinced me the guy was nuts! So, my paranoia subsided enough to drive home, but for months I continued to leave my computers, tablets, phones, and other devices in my car whenever I was not using them.

I read that even Mark Zuckerberg covers his cameras with tape, so I did that on all my phones, tablets, and computers.

Cyberattack Chess

My LG V10 phone was compromised many times. Sometimes I could hear clicks in the background trying to crack my passcodes when I was turning the phone back on, even though I used a screen lock and a password-protected encrypted SIM card. Often the app icons were moved around on the screen after I powered up. I lost many texts, and many others were delayed. I received a text that one of the deacons of my church had died that morning—two days later. A text from my neighbor Rick offering me his season tickets to see the University of Tennessee Lady Vols play basketball that night didn't arrive until the next day. Sometimes a dozen or so texts would arrive at one time from the previous day or so.

After each security breach, I devoted lots of my time to figuring out how they'd done it, and either plugging up the holes or reversing the damages. Meanwhile, Elijah suggested I just ignore the attacks, breaches, and disruptions. "If you play with fire, you will get burned!"

I used the fact that whoever was hacking my phone read my text messages to tell my cyber enemies about Jesus. Sometimes I would send them text messages by addressing them in messages to myself, which they undoubtedly read. In most of the messages, I told them I was praying for them and either told them about Jesus (John 3:16) or gave my personal Christian testimony. I prayed that some of them would become Christ followers, and their experience would lead to a Great Awakening throughout the crime ring.

I got so frustrated with my V10 smartphone that near the end of 2017, I mailed it to Jaylin, a tech guy who'd reinstalled its Android software a few times, just to get it out of my house. I didn't even want to see it again. Now *that* was a manic thing to do!

A month or so later, I met Jaylin at a Dunkin' Donuts in Charlotte and gave him other phones I'd bought along the way (except for my Samsung J7) and a bunch of my tablets and laptops. I was sick of the stuff tearing up and wasting so much of my time trying to fix it. A few months later, I figured out how the V10 was probably being hacked and taught that trick to Jaylin. I wished I hadn't given that expensive phone away.

I saw many other types of malicious shenanigans, but I'll only describe a few.

Wi-Fi and Internet Service Breaches

At night, many lights on my router/modem would flash on and off, showing a lot of access to my home internet service. Disconnecting all of my devices didn't make a difference. I researched and found out that hackers search for high-speed services with unlimited cycles to improve the chances of not being noticed. They sell their fraudulent internet service to their customers, who usually don't know the internet resources were stolen. They often use these private services at night while the owner is sleeping. Often, several services are bundled together with software that seamlessly switches between systems.

In late 2017, I found out about the Wi-Fi vulnerability KRACK (Key Reinstallation Attack) that compromises the WPA2 Wi-Fi Protected Access protocol that's supposed to secure Wi-Fi connections. Feeling helpless, I dropped my internet and cable service for a year. I wasn't able to watch TV, except on the two channels where I could get reception using rabbit ears. I could access the internet through my smartphone (when it was operative, and

I wasn't afraid to use it), or for the thirty-minute time limit at a nearby library. I didn't access the internet again using home Wi-Fi until September 2018, after I had given up fighting my technology cyberwar. Of course, I didn't use public Wi-Fi, because those services were the most susceptible of all to hacking.

Facebook Hacks

In 2017, at the same time I dealt with all of these technology problems, I also had a lot of issues with Facebook, especially with false profiles using the name of one of my friends, often with a blank picture or an actual photo of them they'd found somewhere, and usually having some mutual friends. Hackers are slick! Sometimes they would ask me to friend them on Facebook or Facebook's Messenger app, or just send me a link that would have infected my phone or computer with malicious malware, such as viruses and ransomware, had I clicked on it.

I began trying to find my cyber lover, Bill Moore. I didn't find him, but I blocked all profiles that came up with the names Bill Moore or William Moore. The next day, or sometimes immediately thereafter, a bunch of new profiles would pop up with the same names.

When I would deactivate my Facebook account, it would almost instantly be reactivated. Once I got a message, ostensibly from Facebook, asking me to upload a picture of my driver's license held beside my face and using a link they provided. I did it, and immediately a black screen came up with a one-line, mysterious error message. I was in an office where I was a volunteer, which used AT&T internet service. I heard noises that could have been pings of the online printer. My iPhone 4s, which had never been used there, mysteriously joined their network—which had a long, obscure password of letters and numbers. How could I not have a "Twilight Zone" moment?

Many techy people validated several of my claims. My friend Mark, who has a PhD in Computer Science, told me he believed everything I said was possible. He even went so far as to suggest I start a cybersecurity consulting firm, because I had learned so much from playing "cyberattack chess" with my opponents. A cybersecurity expert at AT&T told me he knew how to do a lot of the things I was seeing, but he was prohibited from telling me by his employment agreement.

You don't need to believe any of these experiences to conclude that, given I believed they were real hacks, it's surprising that I didn't suffer a psychotic break before I did.

House at Pooh Corner

But I've wandered much further today than I should.

—"House at Pooh Corner" (a composition by Kenny Loggins)

Meet My Winnie-the-Pooh Bear

To completely lay the foundation for the psychotic experience I had in 2018, I'm compelled to explain how the end of a close friendship contributed to its onset.

My psychologist, whom I'd been seeing since the late 1980s (Mr. Ed, I affectionately called him), maintained that each of my psychotic episodes in the 80s and the one in 1995 were triggered by a rejection by a significant man in my life, usually my ex-husband Steve. Mr. Ed said that my 2018 psychotic episode—the first hospitalization in 23 years—had been instigated by the recent experiences in my relationship with my friend I'll call Winnie.

What happened to our friendship? A stranger at Covington Fellowship Church put it best on August 5, 2018, when she prophesied that she was seeing a *Christopher Robin* situation in my life. She was referring to the end of the A. A. Milne Winnie-the-Pooh stories, in which Christopher Robin says goodbye to Winnie-the-Pooh and states they will not see each other again. In any case, the stranger was right—though the analogy fails in the sense that it's not clear who rejected whom.

What I do know is that my obsession with making sure Winnie became a believer in Jesus Christ finally shattered a close friendship of twenty-eight years.

Winnie was the first man I dated after my divorce from Steve in 1990. We found each other on the local daily newspaper's dating matchmaker page. We met at a Shoney's for our blind date. I don't know what I was thinking, but I wore a gypsy boho skirt with a magenta and black background and a multicolor zigzag print design. My black silk blouse sported a tarnished bronze, vintage, art déco style bodice necklace that clashed with my big, colorful, dreamcatcher, dangling earrings. If this doesn't sound hideous enough, I can't even describe my black plastic sandals with a big toe separator, connected to my foot with a wide, magenta shoestring that threaded the shoe bottom, crisscrossed around my leg, and tied in a bow halfway up my leg. Winnie later said my gypsy look was the crowning detail that attracted him to me.

Since I am gullible, I think it was his big whopper lies that drew me in, like his former tag team professional wrestling career and his experiences as a masseur when he lived in Hawaii—where, incidentally, I'd purchased my sandals and a matching white pair with five neon colors of interchangeable shoe strings. I think this is all that needs to be said about the beginning of our relationship to explain why we were so well-suited.

Winnie and I dated for about a month before I *friend-zoned* him. You usually never hear back from a guy after that relegation, but not Winnie. We remained close friends until February 2018.

When my children were small, they'd ask, "Mommy, why don't you marry Winnie?" How do you explain to a child, "Yes. Winnie is good to us, fun to be with, and makes us laugh, but he and I have different ideas about how to manage money!"

Winnie and I went Dutch to lunch or dinner, and sometimes both, almost every day after Alan moved to Virginia in 2013. For the first twenty-three years of our friendship, we had dinner and saw a movie every Friday night, except during the six years he was married to Andrea, or when one of us was dating someone, or when I was too disabled to go. When my health permitted, we might go to a Lady Vols basketball game, drive to the Smoky Mountains to see the beautiful colors of fall's changing leaves, window shop and eat at the Pancake Pantry in Gatlinburg, or get some bargains at the outlet stores in Pigeon Forge.

OCD (Obsessive Conversion Disorder)

The obsession with making sure Winnie became a Christ follower began early in our relationship. It intensified after the death in 2001 of his only child, Bob, from a blood clot to his lung, following an appendectomy. Bob's dying words were "Make sure Pops gets saved!"

If one of my children had said that, I would have dropped to my knees and prayed to Jesus to forgive my sins and save me from eternal damnation and separation from God. But not Winnie. He remained a professed atheist throughout our friendship. At the time of Bob's death, Winnie's only relatives were his two grandsons, Michael and Brandon (ages eight and four, respectively) and his daughter-in-law Mia, so I believed it my sole responsibility to make sure Bob's dying wish came true.

I feel so much guilt about the way I approached Winnie with my mission. As someone with bipolar disorder and a variable relationship with Jesus Christ, I fueled his opinion of Christians as hypocrites. When I had a close relationship with Christ, I tried not to beat him over the head with a Bible! Any time the subject came up, I answered his objections and presented the gospel (the good news about Jesus Christ) to him in as many unique ways as I could think of. I know he was interested, or he wouldn't have brought the subject up sometimes and talked with me about it so much. I don't like to debate religion, but I was patient even though he was argumentative, trying his best to sway me to his way of thinking. So many of his statements were blasphemous, but I endured them, thinking he would finally change his mind.

I prayed for salvation for Winnie often, almost every day, for the last few years of our friendship. I asked my spiritual mentor, Betty, to put him on her prayer list. She is the most ardent prayer warrior I know. Her daughter Maria once told me that her mother was like the IRS. The only way to get off her prayer list was to die. And that wasn't foolproof! She prayed for a paraplegic, nonbeliever friend I'd asked her to pray for in the 90s up until eight years after he died. I didn't know he had died until one day I was curious and searched for his obituary, which stated he had been an assistant pastor of a nearby Church of Christ congregation. Betty's prayers were powerful and effective.

I'd Die for My Friends

There is no greater love than to lay down one's life for one's friends.

—John 15:13 (NLT)

In July 2017, I had breakfast with Winnie and his grandsons at an IHOP. I told them about Jason, the 37-year-old son of close friends, who had died five years earlier from colon cancer. Knowing he was dying, Jason had asked his pastor to not eulogize him, but to tell the mourners about Jesus Christ instead. Jason was very popular, and he knew lots of his young, nonbeliever friends would attend his funeral, and that might be their only chance to hear the gospel message.

The sanctuary was packed. At the end of the service, the pastor asked us to repeat a prayer for salvation after him if we wanted to have a relationship with Jesus, like Jason did. Then he asked people to raise their hand if they had prayed that prayer. Jason's father told me later that there were well over one hundred people that got saved that day!

I told Michael and Brandon about telling Winnie I would gladly die if I knew he and some of my family members I'm concerned about would get saved at my funeral. Winnie flashed a cunning smile and, with a twinkle in his eye, said something like, "You'd be surprised!" Given his whimsical personality, that made me believe he had gotten saved after I'd told him I would die for him, and that he just hadn't told me. I believed it for a few days and was shocked when I referenced his salvation a few days later, only to find out I had misunderstood. I was disappointed and visibly upset. I cried and expressed my displeasure. As usual, he didn't say anything back.

Demon or Delusion?

After I began having serious hacking issues with my cellphones and computers in the fall of 2017, on October 11 I stopped by Winnie's house to borrow his old laptop. After I'd been home for about an hour, he came over to ask me to go to dinner with him. As we were talking, I complained about something my former scammer lover, Bill Moore, had said during a Google Hangout. I'd sent him a recording I'd made at my church of my late friend Mary singing "There's Power in the Name of Jesus." Bill had repeated the title in a mystical-sounding voice and told me that the recording had moved him to tears, and he had gotten out his Bible (on the oil rig) and read from it. Since I doubted whether that was true, given his other lies, I indicated to Winnie how offended I had been.

Then Winnie said, in a spooky voice that was not his own, "I like the old-fashioned gospel hymns myself, like 'Jesus and the Twenty-Pound Hammer.'"

I felt the Holy Spirit saying,

Don't cast your pearls before swine.
Don't waste what is holy on people who are unholy.
Don't throw your pearls to pigs!
They will trample the pearls, then turn and attack you (Matt. 7:6 [NLT]).

The freaky voice frightened me, and I said something about needing to get ready for my trip to Charlotte to visit my family the next day. As I walked Winnie to the door, he asked again, in his normal voice, about going to dinner. He told me later that he didn't remember coming to my house that night.

I did my laundry to get ready for my trip, but I was afraid to be alone in my house. I left for Charlotte at about 4:30 a.m. I don't see well at night. I was probably traveling about 40 mph on I-40. Tractor trailer trucks were flashing their lights and blowing their horns at me. The "demonic voice" made my paranoia and mania worse, which later made Elijah and Nicole question if I had truly been healed. Elijah used air quotes around *healed*, and I was both humiliated and heartbroken.

Remission and Relapse

In late October 2017, Winnie became deathly sick. A woman who was to clean his house found him in bad shape and called Mia. Mia called me and asked me to go to his house to see if we should call 911. Winnie was so swollen, he could barely breathe. Before they put him into the ambulance, the EMT indicated to me that he was in critical condition. I couldn't go to the hospital. I was a basket case. I couldn't bear to watch a close friend die and go to hell.

The next morning, I received a text from Winnie's phone asking me where I was.

Assuming it was from one of his family members, I asked who was texting me. The text response said it was Winnie, and he asked me if I could come to the hospital and bring his teeth.

I told him I would not cross a dangerous four-lane highway during rush-hour traffic to get his false teeth, but I did leave immediately to visit him.

Much to my surprise, he appeared to be healed. He was sitting up in bed. He had cleaned his plate, which had contained food he hadn't been able to eat in months because of his stomach problems. Before, he would only eat small amounts of soft foods.

Then came the best news of all. Because of his miraculous healing, Winnie said he had asked God to forgive him and had become a Christian in the middle of the night while he was getting an MRI. I believed him and was elated.

Winnie's healing definitely appeared to be real. When his physical therapists came in, they got him up, and he walked, with the aid of a walker, the entire circle around the hospital floor. I discussed Winnie's miracle with his doctor, who agreed it was unexplainable in the natural realm.

When I got home, I texted photos and a short video to Mia, his grandsons, and some of my nonbeliever relatives and friends, whom I'd hoped would become Christians after seeing the evidence of a true miracle.

I came back to the hospital the next day and found Winnie sick again. I couldn't believe it! When Mia called to congratulate him on his healing and salvation, I heard him tell her that he wasn't healed, and the salvation experience wasn't true, either. He said he'd been teasing me. He'd just told me what he thought I wanted to hear.

I was furious! I got up from my chair, raised my voice and expressed my disgust, and left the room—not to come back.

I spent the next two weeks in Charlotte, so it was easy to pause our relationship. No apologies came, only a text saying I'd left my jacket at the hospital and could come get it when I got back to town. I never picked the jacket up. I chalked it up to a minor loss.

There might have been a couple of casual, "How's the weather over there" type of phone calls after that. I tried to explain why I needed to chill on our friendship for a while, to try to process what had happened. Later, my pastor told me Satan can't heal anyone, but he can make it look like someone was healed for a short period.

Running off the Rails

*It is the duty of the human understanding to understand that
there are things which it cannot understand.*

—Søren Kierkegaard

Gulliver's Travels

Sometime after my 1982 psychotic break, I read Barbara Gordon's 1979 memoir, *I'm Dancing as Fast as I Can*. An addiction to a prescribed drug (Valium), and a therapist's bad advice to quit cold-turkey, led to a mental state that caused her life to spin out of control.

Her book's title is an apt description of what I was experiencing in 2017 and the first half of 2018, all leading up to the psychotic breakdown. During that time, I skittered around like a jackrabbit, dividing my time between my home in Knoxville, Megan's family home in Charlotte, and Elijah's home in Chicago and later Charlotte, after his family moved there in July 2017. I spent only about 55 percent of my time at my home in Knoxville in 2017 and approximately 70 percent in 2018. I flew to Chicago twice during that time, staying a total of five weeks. I babysat, cleaned, folded laundry, often washed dishes, and, on my last trip there, I packed some moving boxes and spent two nights in a hospital with heart attack warning symptoms. It was just a stomach virus. Elijah remarked that, given my health history, they would have admitted me, even if I only had symptoms of a common cold.

In addition to my Chicago visits, I drove to Charlotte (250 miles one-way) twelve times by myself to visit Elijah, Megan, and their families during 2017 and 2018. The last two trips to Charlotte were after my severe manic psychotic breakdown in mid-2018.

In mid-October 2017, I made a long road trip from Knoxville to Harrogate, Tennessee to Middlesboro, Kentucky, then back to Knoxville and on to Charlotte and back to Knoxville—a total of 675 miles in eight days.

My credit card was suspended for a brief period, because they suspected it had been stolen, since I used it in multiple states during a short amount of time. In four days, I made purchases in Knoxville, Middlesboro, and back in Knoxville, but my purchase was declined the next day in Charlotte. It's good to know they monitor my card so closely.

A Homeless Houseguest

Near the end of November 2017, in the midst of my battles with the cyberattackers, I did something that surely would have worried my daughter-in-law, Nicole—if she'd found out about it. Nicole tries to keep an eye on me, and she would have considered this incident a sign of poor judgment and unpredictable behavior that could trigger a severe manic episode.

I found a man named Tom walking near the church I was attending that day. It was about 30 degrees Fahrenheit outside. He was wearing a T-shirt and a windbreaker and shoes that were much too big for him. Tom was homeless and had just been released from a nearby hospital. His discharge notes indicated he was awaiting surgery to remove a cancerous tumor in his right lung that was the size of a softball.

Tom came inside the church with me and, later, I took him to a nice restaurant and to a Walmart, where I bought him shoes, a coat, and other warm clothing. I didn't know what to do with him, so I took him home with me until I could find a better plan.

He slept in my den four nights on double stacked air mattresses. Each day Tom sat with me all day long at my dining room table, drinking endless cups of coffee, and listening, without interrupting, to detailed stories about my life. On the third day, he remarked that he'd listened to many homeless people who were as high as they could be on crystal meth, and were extremely energetic and talkative, but he added, "I've never met *anyone* who can talk as much as you do!"

Tom told me he used to be an alcoholic, but had quit drinking. I suspected, and it was later confirmed, that this was far from the truth. I believe he was self-medicating to deal with a mental illness, probably bipolar disorder or schizophrenia, based on our conversations. He'd led me to believe that his surgery was to be on Friday of that week, but after I read his hospital discharge summary while he was asleep, I realized his surgery was not yet scheduled. I became irritated and troubled—and worried about the direction my mental health was heading. I'd been duped. When I confronted him about these misrepresentations early Thursday morning, he apologized and said he would leave. I offered to cook breakfast first, but he wanted to leave right then. He left on foot in the darkness.

After that, he called a few times, but I would not meet him anywhere because I didn't want to get in a situation where I might get hurt. So why did rational thinking about risk and danger finally set in? I believe my hypomania had abated.

The Greater Gifts

In late December 2017, I learned that I seem to have a spiritual gift to pray for healing. I planned to drive to Charlotte on December 21 to spend Christmas with my family. I'd had dull chest pain and weakness the entire week preceding. Because of my heart disease and the quadruple bypass surgery I had in 2009, my doctors want me to go to the ER any time I have chest pains or other symptoms of a heart attack. But I wouldn't go to the ER this time, because I didn't want to risk missing Christmas. Poor logic, but real nonetheless.

About 3:00 a.m. on December 20, I felt a prompting by the Holy Spirit to turn on the Testament of Truth TV (TTTV) Christian TV station. The program was almost over. The hosts were interviewing Todd White, an internationally known pastor, evangelist, and healer. He was a peculiar-looking Caucasian guy with dreadlocks to his waist. Before he became a Christ follower, he had been a drug addict and atheist for 22 years. They showed videos of him at the Temple Mount praying for healing and talking about Jesus to Jews and Muslims alike. Todd definitely has charisma and a special anointing for healing and evangelism.

At the end of the broadcast, the hosts asked Todd to pray for the prayer requests that had been submitted during the show. This program heavily influenced the delusions of my impending manic psychotic episode.

Later that day, I ran several errands and delivered Christmas presents to some friends. At the last house I visited, the chest pain turned into a stabbing pain on the right side of my chest. My friend could see the grimace on my face each time I felt a sharp pain. Her husband had Alzheimer's, so she couldn't leave him, but she said if I didn't go to the ER, she would call her daughter to take me.

I drove myself. By the time I got to the ER, I was convinced I was dying. I had never been scared any of the other times I'd been to the ER with chest pains. I felt safe there. But *this* pain was intense. Identifying with the character of Fred G. Sanford (played by Redd Foxx) from the 1970s sitcom *Sanford and Son*, I thought to myself, "Elizabeth, this the big one!"

My EKG matched the previous ones in my record. They sent me to the lobby to wait. Next, they X-rayed my lungs and brought me back to the lobby again. I texted Nicole to tell her where I was and that I might have to FedEx their Christmas gifts. She told me not to worry about them.

Then I texted my friend Alma and asked her to call a young guy named CJ who worked at an IHOP I frequented in Charlotte. He'd asked me to bring him a homemade cheesecake to give to his girlfriend. He'd jokingly said he thought she'd marry him if he gave her a cheesecake. I seemed to worry more about CJ than not being with my family on Christmas! More twisted logic.

Then I remembered keeping my mom alive one time by holding her hand and quoting the 23rd Psalm over and over when the doctors said she wouldn't make it through the night. She lived a year or so after that. So, I tried repeating that psalm. My pain was still intense.

Then I thought, *maybe I should pray using some of the words I heard Todd White say*. I did, and immediately the pain stopped! When they put me into a room, I told the nurse my pain was gone. She tried to placate me with an insincere, "Yes. Sometimes prayer helps."

The ER doctor released me at midnight, saying all the tests showed I hadn't had a heart attack, but I should follow up with my doctor in a week or so. The next morning at 9:00, I left for Charlotte.

On the Monday after I returned to Knoxville from Christmas break, my PCP's nurse called and said, "Dr. M wants you in here as soon as possible."

I replied, "But I didn't have a heart attack."

The nurse said my doctor had some reason for the urgency.

I went the next day. The doctor showed me that his report said I had an unknown mass in my right lung. The mass in the X-ray image was large and on the side where I'd had intense pain. The ER staff had conjectured that it might be pneumonia. But I hadn't even had a cold in a long time. My X-ray was not mentioned anywhere in the discharge notes the ER department had given to me.

My PCP said, "You know I'll have to do another X-ray."

On the new X-ray, there was no mass anywhere in my lung. The doctor asked if I was disappointed that he couldn't tell me what the mass was.

I told him, "Well, look at it this way. I didn't have a heart attack. I don't have pneumonia. There's no mass in my lungs. What else do I need to know?"

He smiled in agreement.

Power and Love

Emboldened by my healing, I began learning about Todd White's ministry at LifestyleChristianity.com and registered to attend two Power and Love (P&L) Christian events in 2018, one in February in Orlando and one in May in Winston-Salem.

The P&L events were dynamic and emotionally charged. As part of the conferences, we would do outreach to strangers during the lunch and dinner breaks, usually going in small groups, but since I would tend to do all the talking, I usually preferred to go alone. I would talk to strangers, give them my personal healing testimony, if appropriate, and ask if they'd like me to pray for anything. Sometimes it was for healing. I brought some easy-to-read version (ERV) Bibles I'd bought to give to homeless people in Knoxville, and I gave several away at the P&Ls.

I heard Todd White say at a private donor breakfast in Orlando that he didn't think he could afford to eat out if he couldn't afford to tip 100 percent. If you just eat out half as much, you could come out slightly better, because you would only tip 100 percent on one meal.

So, after February 2018, I started tipping 100 percent everywhere—including fast-food restaurants—until I found out I could be getting them into trouble. I would explain my reasoning and ask everyone I tipped to look up Todd White. That was my way of telling them about Jesus Christ.

I was certainly dancing as fast as I could during the long road trips to these two P&Ls.

In February 2018, I took a long circuitous route to the event in Orlando, then on to Charlotte after the P&L. On this two-week road trip, I drove over 2,000 miles. I stayed in Charlotte an additional two weeks before returning to Knoxville.

In mid-April 2018, I drove to Charlotte for the birthdays of two of my granddaughters, Madison and Calypso. I stayed there six weeks before driving to Winston-Salem for the second P&L event. The drive from Charlotte to Winston-Salem to Knoxville included detours in Virginia. I logged 440 highway miles in one week on this trip.

At this point, I can hear Hilda, loud and clear, screaming, "DANGER! DANGER, Will Robinson!"

Return to Pooh Corner

Back to the Days of Christopher Robin and Pooh

—"House at Pooh Corner" (a composition by Kenny Loggins)

Reconciliation

As I was leaving church on a Sunday in early February 2018, I thought about how I used to call Winnie after the service, and we would meet for lunch, often at a new restaurant he'd recently discovered. I missed our conversations about culture, science, history, and technology he'd learned about from watching the National Geographic, Discovery, and History channels. He was especially fond of talking about nanotechnology and religious documentaries, especially if they contradicted my Judeo-Christian beliefs—like denial of a virgin birth or insistence that Jesus and Mary Magdalene were married, or at least lovers. Winnie also spent a lot of time watching Animal Planet and taught me about the habits, habitats, and other facts about weird, unique animals throughout the world.

I definitely missed spending time with Winnie. Knowing he was too sick to drive or eat out, I decided to make a nice meal for him soon.

His grandson Brandon brought him over. I put on the dog! Candlelight, china and crystal, gazpacho, baked Alaskan salmon and veggies in parchment paper, palate cleanser—the whole shebang! Winnie couldn't eat much, but Brandon ate heartily. He even ate all the spicy sushi platter I had picked up at the local Publix (everything else was home cooked).

On a whim, I asked Winnie if he would like to go with me on vacation next week. I planned to spend a week at a beach near Orlando before the upcoming Lifestyle Christianity Power and Love (P&L) event there. Winnie and Brandon were shocked when I invited him, but Brandon said it was a great idea. Winnie said he would ask his home nurse if he was well enough to go.

The home nurse said no, but Winnie went anyway. I ignored God's warning to not cast my pearls before swine.

P&L Road Trip Gone Wrong

The vacation as a whole was a disaster. Winnie wanted to go to a beach in Jacksonville, Florida, so I gave in, as I usually did. But I mistakenly booked a condo in Atlantic Beach near Jacksonville, North Carolina, instead. I realized my mistake early the next morning, but the vacation rental company Vrbo wouldn't give me my money back or let me reschedule for Florida. So we went to Atlantic Beach, turning what was supposed to have been a 1,400-mile round trip from Knoxville to Orlando into a trip to Atlantic Beach, to Orlando, then Charlotte, driving the first 2,000 miles of the trip within fourteen days. This was a lot of miles to drive for a 67-year-old who had only started driving again about four years earlier.

The vacation went reasonably well until we were on our way from Atlantic Beach to Orlando. We spent the night with my brother and his wife in Savannah, Georgia, to break up the ten-hour trip. The next day—which happened to be my birthday—we headed to Orlando. But Winnie was constipated. He had me stop every few exits so he could try to poop. He would stay in the bathroom for long periods of time.

Winnie left his phone on the console in my car during his bathroom stops, so I saw that he was receiving pornographic text messages and photos throughout the day. I was already aware of Winnie's pornography addiction.

His computer, which I had borrowed in October 2017, behaved erratically and then locked up when I tried to remove the pornographic images and videos stored on it. Pornography websites are often a source of viruses and malware, especially if you download photos and files.

We had one legitimate stop for lunch at a Cracker Barrel on that drive to Orlando. During one of Winnie's two long stays in the bathroom there, I prayed for him to be healed of back pain and constipation. When he returned to the table, I asked him to check his back pain. He indicated it was about one out of ten. I was elated!

Counting lunch and the bathroom breaks, it took us eight hours to make what should have been a four-hour trip. I barely got to the P&L event in Orlando on time. There was no time to drop Winnie off at the hotel.

I was overjoyed, because I thought he would go inside the meeting with me and maybe get saved. But no! He moved a chair outside a bathroom and sat there for four hours in case he needed to use it.

When the event was over, I found Winnie.

About that time, Megan called to wish me a happy birthday. I told her about Winnie's healing, but he interrupted me to say his pain level was about an eight. So much for a miraculous healing, bringing about a salvation experience. I was sorely disappointed once more.

Pressure Cooker Explodes

After the long day, I was totally out of it by the time we got back into the car. Winnie was giving me driving directions to the hotel. I was about to explode, but I kept my cool until he got us onto a toll road. When I went through a toll exit with no change, I saw the word *fine* on a sign and freaked out! I got back on the toll road. There was no traffic that late.

I started screaming and drove erratically for a short distance, yelling, "You should never ride with a Christian who doesn't care whether she lives or dies!"

There was no response from Winnie, except for silence. That was not at all surprising. Winnie was placid. He would just clam up and keep his attitudes and feelings to himself. Winnie never seemed to feel any guilt or regret—even when he did something awful. He expressed no feelings of sadness or pity for people he had hurt. There were never any apologies, at least not sincere ones. He showed no remorse for anything he had done or the inconvenience he had caused me that day, especially on my birthday!

I'd planned for Winnie to fly home after we arrived in Orlando, though I hadn't discussed this with him. But I'd had enough. I was at the end of my rope! I got off the toll road, stopped at an abandoned building near a railroad track, and called Frontier Airlines to book a flight home for Winnie the next morning.

I lost it, and told him about the incident with his "devilish" voice in October 2017, before I'd left for Charlotte. I prayed for demons to leave both of our bodies. Then I started singing hymns of praise, because I'd been told demons would flee if you prayed or praised God.

When we got to the hotel, Winnie took the bed, and I was going to sleep in the bathtub. He had taken the bed in Greensboro on our way to Atlantic Beach, and I'd slept in the recliner. But this was a cheap hotel and there were no recliners, just a couple of straight-back chairs. And there was no tub, only a walk-in shower, so I decided to try to sleep in my car. Winnie always expected that I would put myself out to help him, and I always dutifully obliged.

Before I left the room, I exploded again, telling Winnie a bunch of stuff that I'd wanted to say for twenty-eight years. I'd kept it bottled up inside because I didn't want to hurt his feelings or jeopardize our friendship. I'm sure I scared him half to death.

> You're the most selfish person I've ever met! Don't you ever tell me again that Megan is selfish.
> Did you treat your mother like this? What about your other friends and five ex-wives?
> I should have listened to the Holy Spirit when he told me to not cast my pearls before swine after hearing that eerie devilish sounding voice coming out of your mouth blaspheming Jesus!

When I got to my car, I was so upset. I shouldn't have said all those negative things to Winnie. That was atypical for our relationship. I'd never said a cross word to him in our entire relationship. But tonight, it was as if I were a venting pressure cooker. I was sure I would have to check myself into a local mental hospital.

I started praying. I knew I needed sleep. I asked God what to do. The car wasn't comfortable enough for sleeping in my current mental state. Should I rent another room? It was about four hours before Winnie needed to be at the airport for his early flight. I left a voicemail for Elijah to call me, but he was on shift in the ER at the hospital.

The solution came to me, and I was at peace after that. I marched up to the room, woke Winnie up, and in a quieter voice asked him if he wanted me to call an Uber to take him to the airport now, or if he would prefer to sleep in the car. He chose the latter and left me in the room.

I fell asleep immediately.

When I got to my car the next morning, Winnie was asleep. I sincerely apologized for the night before and told him I cared for him. He said he accepted my apology, but judging from his demeanor, I could tell he hadn't. I took him to the airport and gave him $40 for breakfast and cab fare home.

After breakfast at a Wawa near the airport, I returned to the church where the P&L was being held, determined to enjoy my time there without Winnie.

Hilda's Harbingers

The moan of the whip-poor-will from the hillside;
the boding cry of the tree-toad, that harbinger of storm;
the dreary hooting of the screechowl

—Washington Irving, *The Legend of Sleepy Hollow*

January 3–May 23

Precursors

By the time 2018 rolled around, I was already experiencing warning signs of mania: the paranoia and obsession with the cybersecurity issues, the many solo road trips, the perceived miracle in the ER in late December 2017, etc., so I was already in a precarious mental state.

While the disastrous trip with Winnie and resulting rejection may have been the main trigger for my hypomania, moderate mania, and eventual psychosis in mid-2018, many of the risk factors contributing to my psychosis had started before the trip to Orlando. They could probably have been detected by Hilda, the wearable robot companion—even though they were subtle and unrecognized by those around me.

A Second Miracle?

January 3

On the morning of January 3, 2018, before I left Charlotte to go back to Knoxville, my two-year-old grandson, Ethan, was nestled in his mother Nicole's arms on the living room couch. He'd developed a high fever overnight and was crying uncontrollably, combined with a continuous, barking cough.

I walked over to the couch and pushed back his little curls so I could feel his hot forehead. As I did, I prayed silently, imitating in my head the first part of the prayer for healing I'd heard Todd White pray on the TTTV Christian TV network. I left the room and finished the prayer in my head when I sat down in the den beside my granddaughter, Madison, to watch her play a video game. Almost immediately, Ethan quit crying and coughing. He was the first person, besides myself, for whom I'd prayed for healing.

I waited for several minutes before returning to the living room to check on him. He was sitting on Nicole's lap, eating a breakfast bar. I commented about that to Nicole, and she told me that was his third one. Later she told me it was like a miracle that he got better so quickly! At this point, I wasn't convinced about his total healing, or that my prayer had anything to do with it, and I feared the denial and ridicule of my family, so I just shrugged my shoulders, flashed a big smile, and said, "Well, I prayed for him."

Red Flags in Tennessee

January 3–15, January 20–February 15

Ethan's ostensible healing fueled my grandiose ideas of being a faith healer. I became somewhat of a healing ambulance chaser, approaching strangers with a cane, walker, wheelchair, or obvious disability to ask if I could pray for them. I remember one woman, sitting in a wheelchair at the Wild Eggs restaurant in Knoxville, turning down my offer to pray for her—but that was the exception rather than the rule.

There were other red flags in early 2018. I had some delusions of personal supernatural healings, such as my attached earlobe miraculously growing to match the unattached one in January and my teeth straightening as I sat in my dentist's office in early February.

The absurdity of the cybersecurity claims made earlier in January by the technical support representative at an electronics retailer amplified my feelings of paranoia and led to more extreme reactions to the security of my devices and internet services.

And on February 7, my elevated mood and poor judgment were what led me to invite Winnie to accompany me on that one-week beach vacation on the way to my first P&L event in Orlando.

Knoxville to Greensboro, Atlantic Beach, Savannah, Orlando, Hilton Head, and Charlotte

February 15–28

By the time of our road trip, I was already hypomanic. My personal interactions with him during the calamitous, long journey pushed me over the edge into what I label a moderate mania mini-episode in Orlando. Maybe if I'd been more stable, as upsetting as the Winnie situation was, it wouldn't have led to the feelings of rejection caused by the loss of a longtime friend, and, ultimately, to the full-blown psychotic episode I experienced in mid-2018.

Outreach in Orlando

February 21–24

After Winnie flew home from Orlando, I continued to pray for strangers during the P&L outreach times and at restaurants and rest stops on my way to Charlotte after the P&L. Sometimes I would give them money if I perceived a need. Once, while hanging out with a small group of homeless people behind a Wendy's in Orlando, I prayed for a restorative miracle to cause a man's leg, which had been severed below the knee in a motorcycle accident, to grow back, but under my breath I prayed: *Please, God, don't let it happen while I'm here, because I know I would freak out!* I sensed he wasn't a Christ follower, but I wasn't confident enough to present the gospel to him, so I gave him my personal Bible with a maroon, zippered, cloth cover case in which I'd inserted $20, marking John 3:16, and challenged him to find it.

I wasn't bold like Todd White. Unless they told me, I would not ask people if they'd been healed. I thought I couldn't face rejection if they'd said no. Though I met most of them only briefly, it was simply enough for me to know that I'd prayed for them, in obedience to the Holy Spirit, without knowing whether they were healed. Sometimes they told me they had been healed, and sometimes I could surmise from their reactions. Sometimes they cried and thanked me. At that time, I had grandiose notions of self-importance and thought almost everyone I prayed for was healed.

Healings at the Northlake Mall

February 28–March 14

For the next two weeks after the P&L, while visiting my children and grandchildren in Charlotte, I frequently went to the Northlake Mall to do Lifestyle Christianity. I prayed for healing for several people, usually presenting the gospel somewhere in my relatively short prayer, but I never followed up to ask them to pray a prayer for salvation.

One of the healing instances stands out. I'll call the women in this story Sarah and Dawn. I spied Dawn, a young woman in her twenties, pushing an older woman, Sarah, in a wheelchair, who appeared to be in her late fifties or early sixties. As I walked toward them, I felt in my spirit that I was supposed to pray for Sarah, but I disobeyed, and just smiled and greeted them. After we passed, I felt convicted to go back. I turned around, but I just walked on past them. After a few steps, I finally got my courage and went back to ask Dawn if I could pray for Sarah. Dawn said she would ask her. As she pushed the wheelchair into a center crosswalk, I closed my eyes and prayed.

Dawn gestured for me to come over. She explained that Sarah had been deaf and unable to speak since birth. We all held hands as I prayed. I opened my eyes and observed a big smile and tears running down Sarah's face. I bent down to her eye level and whispered in her ear, "Jesus loves you!" She cried uncontrollably. I forgot that she wasn't supposed to be able to hear me. I smiled and walked away without verifying whether she was healed.

Back in Tennessee

March 14–April 13

I stayed busy while in Knoxville—doctors' appointments; breakfast, lunch, or dinner with many friends; visits to the homes of church friends; and a two-night stay in a motel in my hometown, fifty miles away, to visit family and random friends I hadn't seen or kept in touch with for a long time. I was talkative and energetic, and I had grandiose ideas about myself. Everywhere I went, I prayed for healing for some of those present or prayed about the prayer requests for others, as we embraced or held hands in a circle. One of my cousins questioned my gift for healing. At one house, there was an acrid odor coming from my armpits, which I couldn't remove by washing with bathroom soap. I was so embarrassed. Steve would always say that was a sign of an impending manic episode. Hilda could have detected this conspicuous harbinger.

I didn't cry or openly grieve the heartbreak of losing my former best friend, Winnie. And I never reached out to him. The only time I saw Winnie after our blowup in February was when he came over in mid-March 2018, after I'd returned from my visit in Charlotte following the Orlando P&L event. His grandson, Brandon, brought him over to get his luggage and the gun and knife that Winnie hadn't been able to take on the plane. They both stayed in his car. Winnie tried to assure me he had forgiven me, but from his uncharacteristic, detached tone of voice, I could tell he still hadn't.

I didn't hear from Winnie again before I left for the second P&L event in Winston-Salem in May 2018, and I didn't reach out to him either. But the feelings of disappointment and rejection, and my sorrow at how this long friendship had ended, stayed with me.

I wasn't feeling much at this time. A disassociation from my emotions often accompanies my hypomania and moderate mania. This was another harbinger that went unnoticed.

Psychosis Risk Factors in Charlotte

April 13–May 23

I remained in Knoxville for a month before driving back to Charlotte for the birthdays of my granddaughters, Calypso and Madison, in April and May.

I spent six weeks in Charlotte, dividing my time between Megan's and Elijah's. My mood was close enough to baseline that my family wasn't concerned. I spent most of my time playing with my grandchildren, often just watching the older ones play video games, sometimes joining in, which really meant holding a controller and pretending to know what I was doing. I didn't fool any of them who knew how to play. I held the younger ones and sometimes sang lullabies and rocked them to sleep. I read books to all of them at bedtime. I babysat and did household chores. And, oh! How could I forget? I changed quite a few diapers!

It was a happy time for me. All of my family members got along well. We played virtual reality and board games, laughed, and had lots of fun. The children were well-behaved, so I was feeling no stress from family relationships.

Near the end of the six weeks, I developed an itchy rash over much of my body. If I'd been staying with Elijah, when I moved to Megan's, she'd jokingly claim I was either allergic to him or had acquired some disease at his house. She'd then feed me antihistamines. I had Benadryl, but she had a favorite she'd give me too. When I went back to Elijah's, Nicole diagnosed me with an allergy to pollen and treated me with a different antihistamine. We all knew that antihistamines can make me very manic, but no one remembered that.

I was taking all of my current medications as prescribed, including the mood stabilizer, lamotrigine. However, at this time, I wasn't taking the antipsychotic drug, quetiapine, which was prescribed by my psychiatrist in 2012 to replace the lithium. I had taken it for a couple of years, but I believed that the quetiapine was causing some symptoms of TDK (tardive dyskinesia). My psychiatrist had disagreed with my claim and refused to replace it with another drug. So I quit seeing him and asked my PCP, Dr. M, to monitor my bipolar disorder. He'd agreed to follow me closely and let me take only the mood stabilizer, lamotrigine, without an antipsychotic.

By the time I left on May 23 for my second P&L event in Winston-Salem, I was beginning to experience some hypomania, probably because of the antihistamine "overdose." I was also obsessing about the cause of my rash. And, of course, the loss of my friendship with Winnie had to be affecting me on some deeper level, though I refused to think about it.

Winston-Salem P&L Event

Bless the LORD, O my soul;
And all that is within me, bless His holy name!
Bless the LORD, O my soul,
And forget not all His benefits:
Who forgives all your iniquities,
Who heals all your diseases,
Who redeems your life from destruction,
Who crowns you with lovingkindness and tender mercies,
Who satisfies your mouth with good things,
So that your youth is renewed like the eagle's.

—Ps. 103:1-5 (NKJV)

May 23–27

Meet Up in Kernersville

May 23

It was a beautiful, sunny day for the one hundred mile drive to Winston-Salem. I couldn't help thinking about the contrast with my trip with Winnie to my first P&L just three months ago. I was determined to put the conflict with Winnie behind me and enjoy this P&L event.

I was anxious to see my childhood friend Betsy, who'd answered my invitation on Facebook to attend this event. I hadn't seen her since our fifteen-year high school reunion in 1984. There had been such a fuss made by many of our classmates, because the reunion was held at a country club with an open bar, that there had been no more reunions…in the Bible belt.

I met up with Betsy and her friend, Julie, about 2:00 on Wednesday afternoon at a Vrbo B&B in Kernersville, the largest suburb of Winston-Salem, about ten miles from the Benton Convention Center, where the P&L was held.

We all gathered in the kitchen while our hostess, Laura, was cooking our evening meal. I was talking 90 miles per hour. No one could get a word in edgewise. My brain was racing. My thoughts were discontinuous and impulsive. I recognized these harbingers of a manic psychotic episode. It was noted, and, at breakfast on Thursday, I asked the others to pray for my manic symptoms to go away and for me to quit talking so much. It turns out the prayers might not have been required. Or what happened at the Benton

Convention Center that day might have been a direct answer to our prayers. Which came first, the chicken or the egg?

Dehydration Harbinger

May 24

The three of us grabbed lunch from a street vendor. Two of us ate the same food, but only I got sick. I vomited so much that afternoon and evening that I became dehydrated. I stood outside a family style restroom and had to go in every few minutes. I kept housekeeping busy, cleaning up my messes.

True to my excessive tipping, I generously gave the housekeepers money and easy-to-read version (ERV) Bibles. Since English was a second language for most of them, they appreciated the Bibles, and one asked me the next day for copies for other family members.

Betsy had driven me to the event that Thursday morning, but she couldn't take me to the B&B, 20 minutes away, until there was a lull in my vomiting, and even then, I barely made it back. They lined a large trash can with a bag and put it beside my bed. I'm sure I was one of Laura's favorite guests. Well, at least I wasn't talking! Every cloud has a silver lining.

At first, I suspected food poisoning. My vomiting stopped before the Friday sessions, so I drove myself to the Benton Convention Center on Friday and Saturday. All day, the restrooms were wet from mopping, and they stank to high heaven from vomit. So, I changed my vote to a contagious stomach virus. Either way, the effect on my mental health was the same. I emptied my stomach and probably had low blood sugar. I missed my meds Thursday night as well as some meals. This contributed to my body and brain getting off balance, but these circumstantial harbingers were beyond my control.

Close Encounters of an Extraordinary Kind

May 26

The rest of my experiences at this P&L followed the pattern of sharing my testimony with strangers, praying for healing, and giving away more Bibles and money, as I'd done at the Orlando P&L I attended in February 2018—all except for one...and it was different by far than anything I'd ever experienced before.

On Saturday evening, at the concluding session of the event, Todd White invited people to come forward for him to pray for them—for salvation, physical healing, or baptism in the Holy Spirit, which involves supernatural phenomena, such as speaking in unknown tongues.

I went forward. I thought if Todd White prayed for me, I would receive a special prayer language for talking with God. But the line was too long, so a few women began praying for me.

A young prophetess came over and prophesied that I would be a spiritual healer, but I would be different from Todd White, who was flamboyant, like a lion, in his approach. I would be more subdued, like a lioness or lamb. Two women, who were watching from a distance, told me they saw tongues of fire come down and hover over me: "They saw what seemed to be tongues of fire that separated and came to rest on each of them" (Acts 2:3 [NLT]).

Not surprisingly, this generated a plethora of harbingers of moderate mania. Elevated mood. Extreme energy. Grandiose ideas and thinking highly of myself. Overestimation of my abilities.

Reconvened at the B&B

May 26–27

I was euphoric as I drove back to Kernersville. I talked with Betsy and Julie about this astounding occurrence. It was difficult to fall asleep. I remember an unusual night vision. Was it a delusion or a dream? I don't know whether I was awake or in some sleep state. My mind was racing. The room felt like it was spinning. I thought I was receiving a blood transfusion from Jesus. This theme was later expanded in a vignette of my extreme manic psychotic episode at a hospital in Tennessee.

Despite these bizarre incidents, by morning my mood had settled down. When I came downstairs with my luggage, I stopped to say bye to Betsy and Julie. I think their assessment of my mood would have been talkative, with a mood somewhere between baseline and hypomania.

Jesus Has Bluetooth

Jesus looked at them intently and said, "Humanly speaking,
it is impossible. But with God, everything is possible."

—Matt. 19:26 (NLT)

May 27

On Friday evening at the Winston-Salem P&L event, I decided to join a group for dinner at the outreach time instead of going alone like I usually did. As we were teaming up, I noticed Maria, a woman closer to my age, standing with a group of younger people in their 40s. She had a delightful, intriguing presence, so I approached the group and asked if I could join them. We had a delicious meal at a nicer restaurant than I'd been dining in that week.

The group bonded, and we later visited and vacationed together a few times before COVID happened. We still stay in touch. Maria lives in Tasmania, and in 2019, she took a side trip from her visit to Texas to see her son and came to South Carolina and Tennessee. We stayed for a few days in an awesome, three-floor cabin high up in the mountains of Pigeon Forge, went to Dollywood, and took in other attractions—including my favorite, Parrot Mountain, which caused me to look around for Alfred Hitchcock when a bunch of small, green and yellow parakeets surrounded me while I was holding a cup of birdseed. I should have known better!

When I reflect upon the qualities of a Christ follower who is filled with the Holy Spirit, I think of my sweet friend Maria: "But the fruit of the Spirit is love, joy, peace, longsuffering, gentleness, goodness, faith, meekness, temperance: against such there is no law" (Gal. 5:22-23 King James Version [KJV]).

It's no mystery why she reacted with such love and compassion for Maurice.

Maurice was a delightful, charming man of slight build, probably in his late 30s, who was homeless. Maria, Kristy, Laura, and Josh met him outside Maria's hotel when they were saying goodbye after the Wednesday evening session of the P&L event. They prayed for him and invited him to come to the Thursday night session. To Maria's delight, Maurice came. After the event, the group bought him a good meal. During the meal, Maurice asked to borrow Maria's phone to call his mom and grandmother, who lived somewhere in South Carolina, to tell them where he was and let them know he was safe. It had been some while since he'd been in contact with them. It seems the rest of his family had totally rejected him. Maria spoke with his grandma for a few minutes and assured her he was okay.

Maria didn't know it at the time, but Maurice was in major trouble of some kind. He came back on Saturday night, presumably in hopes of getting more donations.

Soon after Maria introduced him to me, he told me, "What I need is money." He appeared to be desperate.

I had some money in my purse, but I prefer not to give money to people who ask me for it. I tend to be judgmental, believing it will be used for drugs or alcohol. Sometimes I accompany the person and buy them food, clothing, or other necessities. However, Maurice sounded desperate, so I made an exception and gave him $20.

Later that evening, Maria reluctantly, and apologetically, asked me if I would take Maurice and her to Awake Church the next morning, where Dan Mohler, one of the P&L speakers, would be preaching. She'd been watching his videos for some time and desperately wanted to meet him. I agreed to meet them at 8:30 a.m. in front of the convention center, which was connected to her hotel, and have breakfast before the church service.

We ended up eating at McDonalds. I bought a big breakfast for Maurice, despite him telling me repeatedly that he would rather have the money. Maurice ate like a ravenous wolf. He probably hadn't eaten anything since the meal the group had bought him on Thursday night. Maria told me later that he had asked her for money when I wasn't around, and she'd given him $40.

Maurice was relatively calm until the service took longer than he had expected. He might have thought we would ask for an offering for him, but he didn't indicate that to me. He asked Maria for her phone during the service, but she didn't give it to him. She wanted to have her picture taken with Dan Mohler after the service. Maurice was very antsy. He obviously needed to get in touch with someone. He left the service and used the phone of someone in the lobby.

Maria was in a long line of people waiting to meet Dan, so Maurice and I waited in the lobby. Maurice was fidgety. He kept saying he wished Maria would hurry up.

I wondered, *Why the urgency?*

Finally, Maria arrived, and we headed for the car. Maurice gave me the address of the Citgo where he wanted me to drop him off, and I entered it into Google Maps. When we got to the four-lane highway, he instructed me to turn left, but I turned right, saying I never make left hand turns on busy highways.

He fussed at me, and I was getting irritated. I think I was a little short with him.

I turned right and made a U-turn at the next light. Somehow the GPS lady took us a long way around to get to the Citgo. Maurice was getting more upset by the minute. But because of my mean spirit, secretly I was enjoying his pain. It still didn't dawn on me that he might be in some sort of trouble and had a reason to be there at a specific time. I might have realized this if I'd been closer to my baseline mental state.

I told myself I would never tell anyone what happened next. But after I asked Maria to describe it in an email, I decided people might believe her. I'm quoting excerpts from her email to me about the incident [with permission]:

> During church, he was very impatient to use my phone and to leave, but I wanted to stay and see the Pastor after the service. Eventually, we left the church and headed to the city. Maurice wanted to be dropped off well before the city and asked us to pull over at a service station to let him out. We had already given him our addresses, and we pulled into a car park at the back of a service station. He got out and was gone.
>
> We noticed a few men sitting in a park across the road and wanted to pray for them and ask the Lord if we should go and pray for them personally.
>
> I had on my lap her phone as it was used as a GPS to guide us back to the city. The screen had turned black long before we started to pray. As we had our eyes closed, I could hear voices and opened my eyes. There was a video playing on her phone on my lap. It was some men arguing about something and Ruth indicated to me that this scene was happening behind us. I didn't turn around but recognized the service station. I continued to watch the video for a moment and sure enough, this was happening in front of the closed service station behind us.
>
> We were wondering what to do when Maurice knocked on the window and said, "What are you doing? Get out of here. It is unsafe." I asked him to get in the car and come with us, but he wouldn't. He was concerned about our safety.
>
> We drove off and left Maurice there and as we drove past the service station, there was no sign of these men on the video. They had disappeared. I looked for any camera that may have been in the area and saw none. This service station and car park were run down and looked unused, and there would be no need for cameras to have been installed in the area.
>
> Even though I was a little scared, Ruth didn't seem to be afraid. She was amazing! We drove to a McDonald's closer to the city and talked about this strange unexplained event. To this day, I still don't know how that video came on her phone to warn us of danger. I thank Maurice for coming to warn us as well. I pray for him and expect him to one day knock on my door, a fully restored

and saved man. I can't wait for that. He knew scripture very well, but was in trouble. May Maurice take hold of the love of God and may he fully know the love of his Saviour.[4]

In the McDonald's parking lot, we prayed, thanking God for His protection. I tried to think of ways that video could've played on my phone in the natural realm. I searched on my phone for a copy of the video, but it was not to be found. I thought maybe my Bluetooth was turned on and someone connected to my phone and played it somehow. It was turned off.

We were still in a dangerous part of town. I drove to a McDonald's closer to the Benton Center, and we ate lunch. I talked with a few people at multiple tables and sat in a booth with a young man with some intellectual disability. He became antsy and left when I offered to pray for him.

Believing we'd probably never see each other again, we sat in the parking lot under a shade tree, listening to Christian music, sometimes singing along, and, generally, just bonding. Clearly, the supernatural phenomenon we'd just witnessed was not bothering us, and, on the surface, it didn't appear to be a harbinger of moderate mania for me.

Looking back, I could have thought the video incident was simply a delusion, hallucination, or manifestation of my impending psychosis…except for the fact that Maria saw it, too! And maybe having such a mysterious experience, which had no logical explanation, contributed to my sense of reality fraying in the subsequent days.

So I am left with no explanation, except that Jesus played that video on my phone to warn us. But what happened to the men I saw in my rearview mirror and in the video? They were standing, facing each other, several feet apart, like in a duel. Maurice told us we were in the *hood* when he came out to warn us, but he was nowhere to be seen either when I turned my car around.

God has protected me before in other situations when I ministered to homeless people, but this time takes the cake!

---

[4] Maria Rossiter, email message to Ruth Manning, June 20, 2018.

PART III

AMAZING TREK HOME

Meemaw2

May 27–29, 2018

Respite in Fancy Gap

Which Road Should I Take?

Cheshire Cat: "Where are you going?"
Alice: "I don't know."
Cat: "Then it doesn't matter which road you take!"

—*Alice in Wonderland* by Lewis Carroll (pseudonym
of Charles Lutwidge Dodgson, a mathematician),
1865

May *27–29*

Which Way?

Sunday, May 27

After a long visit at the second McDonald's, I dropped Maria off at the
Benton Convention Center in Winston-Salem around 5:00 p.m. I had made
no plans for what to do next. Presumably I would drive to my home in
Knoxville. It would be a four-hour, 250-mile straight shot on I-40 West. But
my rambling wanderlust somehow just wouldn't let me stay on course.

I started out on I-40 W headed for Knoxville, but when I came to
the interchange with I-77 in Statesville, I saw signs for I-77 S to Charlotte. I
remembered that my granddaughter, Madison, had asked me to come back
to Charlotte when my conference was over. I almost took Exit 152A to merge
onto I-77 S. Had I gone to Charlotte, Elijah could probably have thwarted
my psychotic episode—at least I wouldn't have quit taking my medicine.

Instead of continuing on to Knoxville on I-40 W, I impulsively took
I-77 N to Mount Airy. The sign reminded me of a friend from there whose
father had been a childhood friend of Andy Griffith. Ralph Edwards flew
him to Hollywood as a surprise guest for the taping of "This Is Your Life,
Andy Griffith." I suspect this remembrance influenced one of the vignettes
("Video Game 2: This Is Your Life") in my psychotic episode.

I drove around Mount Airy for quite a while, reminiscing about
episodes of the Andy Griffith Show with Andy Taylor (Andy Griffith),
Barney Fife (Don Knotts), Aunt Bee (Frances Bavier), and Opie Taylor (Ron
Howard) and decided to spend the night there. I looked downtown for a
quaint, nostalgic hotel or bed-and-breakfast. I called two of the B&Bs, but
there was no answer. I'd passed by the Bee's B&B and Aunt Bees [*sic*]
Restaurant on Main Street, but though I was tired and hungry, I was

discombobulated and had difficulty concentrating or making decisions, so I just drove on by. I suspect my blood glucose level was getting too low, in addition to my symptoms of mania.

I stopped at a Circle K convenience store to fill up and use the bathroom. I bought a Nutty Buddy and called Alan from the parking lot. He lives only an hour from Mt. Airy, but he said he wasn't up for a visit the next day. The two teenagers working there gave me directions to places to eat and several hotels (including Hampton Inn, Holiday Inn, and several others) that were right on my way to my "unknown destination," but I just drove past them. Couldn't choose. Just kept on driving.

Once Upon a Midnight Dreary

You are about to enter another dimension, a dimension not only of sight and sound but of mind. A journey into a wondrous land of imagination. Next stop, the Twilight Zone!

—Rod Serling, *The Twilight Zone*

May 27

I left the Circle K about 8:30 p.m., heading north on Andy Griffith Parkway, a four-lane, eleven-mile stretch of US Route 52 that passes through Mt Airy, renamed in 2002 in honor of its favorite son. When I crossed the NC-VA state line, it began raining. Coming down in bucketloads! Hampered by the envelope of green trees and lush foliage on both sides of the highway, combined with the torrent of water pelting my windshield, I passed the exit to Cana, VA because I didn't see the sign in time. I took the next exit, which was about fourteen miles from the point I entered the Parkway.

The sun had set, and it was nearing twilight. I don't like to drive at night, even without a downpour of rain. I saw no signs to indicate lodging or dining in either direction, just a sign pointing to Hillsville to the left and a KOA campground to the right in Fancy Gap. I was so exhausted, hungry, and disoriented, I fancied that maybe I could find a spot to park at the KOA and sleep in my car for a while until the rain subsided. That should be safe enough.

The sign at the fork indicated that Hillsville was about eight miles to the left. Alan had lived there during part of his childhood, so I figured it must be a small town. Turns out it had numerous hotels and restaurants. There was a Motel 6, Red Roof Inn, Hampton Inn, Comfort Inn and others, and even more places to eat, including Shoney's, McDonald's, Aunt Bea's Barbecue, The Mason Jar, Rio Grande Mexican Grill & Cantina, and the Hillsville Diner.

Not knowing any of this, I turned right at the fork and took my chances for the KOA. In retrospect, I'm sure my blood glucose level was dangerously low. All I had eaten that day was an Egg McMuffin, a grilled chicken sandwich, and a Nutty Buddy at the Circle K, where I had given away money I'd kept in a stash-the-cash diaper for safe keeping. Who would look in there? I can't think straight when my glucose level is low. Bewildered, I didn't pray to God for guidance. I just turned right on the promise of a campground. I didn't find a place to pull over to check Google Maps for nearby restaurants and lodging. Based on my later experiences in Fancy Gap, there was a good chance I wouldn't have had cellphone service, anyway.

I had no way to know I would find a motel, restaurant, and a gas station with a convenience store about a mile or so down Fancy Gap Highway. The rain had intensified, and I began to be afraid. It felt like an episode of the *Twilight Zone*. What happened to that woman who was brave enough to sleep in her car at a campground?

I was elated to see a sign on the left with an arrow pointing to the Mountain Top Motel, which was to become my solace for a couple of nights. Before seeing if the motel had any vacancies, I stopped at the Lakeview Restaurant across the road to see if they'd be open on Memorial Day. My heart sank when I saw the sign Closed Mondays, but regained hope when I read a handwritten note taped to the door saying they'd be open from 7:00 a.m. to 2:00 p.m. on Memorial Day.

Mountain Top Motel Collapse

Then Jesus said, "Come to me, all of you who are weary and carry heavy burdens, and I will give you rest."

—Matt. 11:28 (NLT)

May 27

I was as drenched as a duck when I came into the tiny motel lobby. The attendant, Lora, soon appeared at the bullet-proof security window. The cost for a single night's stay was $60.61. A sign said Cash Preferred. I started to go out into that soaking rain to retrieve some diaper cash, but Lora said that wasn't necessary. It would cost the proprietor less than $2 to accept my credit card.

She was an attractive, fiftyish woman with long, ash-blonde hair pulled back into a ponytail. I commented that she looked tired. She confided that her husband had taken her car and money, and the best job she could find was as a full-time clerk and maid for this motel. In return, she got room and board. No salary. The owner gave her no relief time, so she had not left the premises since she started working there.

I told her we'd talk about it the next day. I offered to pray for her. She's a Christian, so she perked up when I asked. I stuck my hands through the small space in the bulletproof window to hold hers while I prayed.

I went immediately to my room (#1), which faced the back of the building. My car was parked nearby, but I was too tired to bring anything inside, notably my bedtime meds. I ate the peanut butter cheese crackers and the breakfast bar I carried in my purse. It didn't dawn on me that I might have a low blood glucose level until a month or so later. Duh! I removed my soaking wet outer garments, collapsed in the bed, and slept for a couple of hours.

By this time, I'd missed three doses of meds in the past four days. The first ones were on Thursday night after I had vomited for eight hours at the Benton Convention Center in Winston-Salem. I missed the second doses Sunday morning. I'd left the B&B in Kernersville, NC, where I was staying, about 7:30 a.m. to pick up Maria and Maurice in front of the convention center at 8:00. I was too rushed to remember to take my meds.

I'd promised my PCP in February 2016 that I wouldn't quit taking my meds, even though I believed I'd been healed of bipolar disorder. But once I reach a certain point in an out-of-control mania, my reasoning skills are thrown out the window. I took one more set of meds on Monday morning, but during that day, I thought it was a bad Christian witness to tell people I had been healed of all my diseases and still take a handful of meds twice a day. After all, at the P&L, my new friend Josh had told me he used to suffer from bipolar disorder, but now he didn't even have to take medicine for it. The power of suggestion can be so strong when your cognitive skills are already shot.

Monday, May 28

When I woke up in the middle of the night, I took a warm shower, even though I didn't have dry clothes to put on.

There was a large fly, resembling a horse fly, buzzing around in the quaint little bathroom with retro fixtures. I sat very still sideways on the commode seat and watched the fly. She landed on the mirror and seemed to be comfortable sharing her small room with a human guest. I watched her little legs move as if she were trying to make something. I was confused. Only spiders make webs. I wondered if flies could think in some primitive sort of way. Was she watching me as closely as I was watching her? I'm just assuming it was a female fly because she was so busy and dainty in her movements. I couldn't pick her up and turn her upside down to examine her parts, though I wasn't sure what I'd be looking for.

Finally, I got tired of watching the fly, but it had given me a totally new respect for flies and a perspective from the fly's point of view. I don't think I could ever kill a fly anymore, no matter how annoying. A fly is some other fly's mother or father and/or kid fly. I know what it's like to love a child and a grandchild. In my befuddled mania, I concluded it would be a sin to kill a fly.

I've heard Todd White talk about listening to the Scriptures while he's exercising or doing other activities which would preclude reading a Bible. I had no cell service in my fanciful little home away from home. Strangely enough, the Mountain Top Motel business card in the drawer of the bedside table advertised Free High-Speed Wireless Internet and had an access code on the back with thirteen digits and letters. My mind was in no shape to try to accurately type in that code.

So I found my Bible Gateway app and selected the King James Version (KJV) translation that I'd already downloaded on my phone. I covered my naked body with a monogrammed blanket, probably from a Holiday Inn liquidation sale, and began listening to Romans 8. Todd had said at the event in Winston-Salem that it was a pivotal chapter in a pivotal book of the Bible.

> There is therefore now no condemnation to them which are in Christ Jesus, who walk not after the flesh, but after the Spirit (Romans 8:1 [KJV]).

I fell asleep, but the narration continued. That chapter is difficult to understand even when awake and sane. I would wake up at key familiar verses. At some point, I changed to the book of Isaiah in the Old Testament. Again, I seemed to wake up to important, recognizable passages. I believed God was waking me up in His timing to teach me what He wanted me to know at that time.

About 4:00 a.m. I put on my partially dry clothes and went to my car to get my luggage. I wasn't afraid. Turns out there was only one other guest. Next day I saw his pickup truck with an NC license plate parked in the front of the motel, but I never saw him. I also brought in the bag with an array of chips that I had taken to the B&B in Kernersville, NC, where Betsy, Julie, and I stayed during the P&L event. After eating a few bags of Cheetos, Doritos, and Lay's Potato Chips, my stomach quit growling, and I was able to fall back to sleep. I slept like a baby until about 10:00 a.m. Fortunately, they were still serving breakfast at the Lakeview Restaurant.

Breakfast at Tiffany's

That is why I tell you not to worry about everyday life—whether you have enough food and drink, or enough clothes to wear. Isn't life more than food, and your body more than clothing? Look at the birds. They don't plant or harvest or store food in barns, for your heavenly Father feeds them. And aren't you far more valuable to him than they are?

—Matt. 6:25-26 (NLT)

May 28

I greeted three couples in the parking lot as they were leaving. I gave them my healing testimony and told them about Todd White. They were jovial and so friendly. By their responses, I could tell they were Christians. The oldest man was taken in by my winning ways. He asked my name and then if I was related to Peyton Manning. I replied, "I am his grandmother."

He quipped that his name was Jimmie Davis, and he was a former governor of Louisiana. I'm gullible. I almost fell for it. When they all laughed, I knew. I checked it out. The other Jimmie had died in 2000 at the age of 101. He was a singer and songwriter, as well as a politician.

The Lakeview served breakfast until 11:00 a.m. I got in just under the wire. I was starving and ordered a big breakfast—two eggs over medium with country ham ($4.75), two biscuits and gravy ($2.50), two pancakes ($3.55), a large orange juice ($1.95), and coffee ($1.50 with free refills), totaling $14.25, plus tax.

But my bank records show I paid $36.23. I'd left a $20 tip. I told my server about hearing Todd White in Orlando saying that he personally doesn't believe he can afford to eat out unless he can tip 100%. I tipped roughly 125%. Reckless and excessive spending is a common symptom of mania. But I had been tipping like that since February 2018, and had usually tipped between thirty to fifty percent before I heard him say that.

During my breakfast experience, I talked with several patrons. Chatty Cathy! When I first came inside, I sensed that the man sitting at the counter next to the cash register was in no mood to talk with me. I asked, "Would you like to hear how I broke out of a nursing home?" But before he could say anything, I knew and just said, "You'd probably not like to be bothered right now and I understand."

He shook his head yes.

I talked with a woman while her husband was in the restroom. I sat down in his seat at her invitation and began telling her my testimony. She was fidgeting and twirling the edge of her collar as I talked. I asked her if I made her uncomfortable.

76

She said, "No. I do that often." I still think she didn't have a relationship with Jesus, and I was making her nervous. She was saved by the bell when her husband returned to the table, and they left. I wish the conversation could have been longer. Maybe both of them could have been saved from eternal separation from God. I still pray that the seed I planted will be watered by someone else and they will grow into a spiritual knowledge of the saving grace of Jesus Christ.

I spoke with the Christian couple sitting in the booth opposite mine and asked them to look up Todd White. Telling folks about Todd is often my witnessing tool, but in this case, I just wanted to tell them about an evangelist whom I thought might become as well known as Billy Graham someday.

I saw a young girl, maybe age nine or ten, sitting on a stool at the counter, eating breakfast with her father. She finished first and became sort of restless. So I took it upon myself to entertain her. I walked over and asked her to use my phone to take a few pictures of me. Then I took a selfie of the two of us together. She is a beautiful girl with big blue eyes, a huge smile to match, and flowing long blonde hair. She told me she had been saved in a revival at her church right before Christmas. It had been too cold to baptize her in the lake, but she was to be baptized in early June. I asked her to pray for my oldest granddaughter, Sara, to be saved. She said she would. I have since promised Nicole that I will not try to proselytize her children.

When I returned to room #1, I napped a bit, but was awake when Lora came by on her break to talk about her life situation. Afterwards, I prayed with her again and gave her my address and phone number. We've corresponded by mail a couple of times. She's never asked me for money, but I sent her $100 to help out. She quit her job at the motel and now takes care of her brother, who had a stroke. In her last Christmas card, she told me she has cancer, so I sent a check for another $100.

It was about 1:00 p.m. and I realized I needed to go back to the Lakeview for lunch before they closed. They were already closing because they'd run out of food. Being open on Memorial Day had been a big deal in Fancy Gap. They made me a to-go grilled cheese sandwich with chips and sweet iced tea anyway. The check was for $4.65, but I gave them $84.65. I got $20 back to tip Lora for cleaning my room. The remaining $60 provided tips for the servers who hadn't been tipped yet and each of the cooks. Everyone working that day at the Lakeview received a tip.

While they were making preparations to close the restaurant, I prayed for healing of back pain for one of the servers and for hearing for another. Both appeared to be healed. Interestingly, all the servers were named some variation of Deborah. One of them corrected me when I called her Debbie. Some people are sensitive about getting their name wrong. Their name is important to them.

The rest of my afternoon was spent making pictures. I went outside my motel room to photograph the grounds and surroundings. My favorites by far were the purple house surrounded with bright purple blooming forsythia shrubs to match and the ceramic chicken with its head cut off that was in a junk pile in the front lawn, along with a set of rabbit ears, a fireplace poker, and many other gems. It was a delightful treasure trove for a junk collector. I thought about asking Lora to call the owner to see if I could purchase the chicken. It was a memorial to what I was feeling at the time. I didn't, but to my surprise, that evening I found a ceramic chicken in the gift shop that was on one side of the Cochran convenience store. It was colorfully painted and had all of its body parts, but I bought it the next day, anyway.

Shoney's Miracles from Heaven

I tell you the truth, anyone who believes in me will do the same works I have done, and even greater works, because I am going to be with the Father. You can ask for anything in my name, and I will do it, so that the Son can bring glory to the Father. Yes, ask me for anything in my name, and I will do it!

—John 14:12-14 (NLT)

Monday Evening, May 28

Despite my huge breakfast, I was hungry again and decided to look for the Shoney's Alan had told me about when I'd called him on Sunday from Mt Airy. Standing outside the motel, I was able to search for it using my phone. Guess where it was? Hillsville—that small town I had misjudged the night before.

Silvia, a server at Shoney's, and I were getting out of our cars at the same time. After idly chatting a bit, I told her I wanted her to be my server. She said she had to clock in first, but she'd like that. It turns out she was the server who needed the tip money most. Amber, the cashier, later told me that Silvia was a single mom with four children who worked three jobs, despite incredible back pain. I had picked the right server.

I asked Silvia if I could pray for healing for her. She told me about her back pain. I prayed, and she was healed. Later, I noticed she was straining to hear me. I asked about her hearing, and she let me pray for that, too. She could barely hold back tears of joy each time she was healed. Maybe word spread among the employees that Silvia had been healed. Another server came over and I prayed for her hearing, too.

That afternoon I had foot and ankle pain that I'd never had before. Since it didn't persist, I knew it must be a *word of knowledge*—someone I would meet would be suffering from that kind of pain.

When I first went to the food bar, a woman about my age with silvery hair was refilling the food trays. The Holy Spirit told me that she was the one. I asked her if she had foot pain. She told me about her painful arthritis. I asked to pray for healing for her, but she declined. At my booth, I silently prayed for her pain, but there was no opportunity to present the Gospel. I had to be satisfied that I had sown a seed.

The ice cream machine was tricky. A large woman dressed in pink was eating at the table beside the ice cream with her husband and son. She told me how to operate the machine. We struck up a conversation, and I ended up sitting at the table beside her son. My ice cream cone melted as we talked.

I discussed my healing testimony with them. Their son suffers from what they labeled as schizophrenia, resulting from a motorcycle accident. He also has PTSD and seizures. He's a former policeman and now works as a security guard. He was packing a gun. His mother mentioned a psychotic episode he'd had while at the church where his brother-in-law was the pastor. He became wild and asked one man to kill another.

His mother said he was demon-possessed, though all three were Pentecostal Christians. Billy Graham, my pastor, and many others say a Christian cannot be demon-possessed, but we can be demonized, a term I use to indicate "influenced by evil spirits or demons." Since I've been accused of not being a Christian because of my behavior during full-blown psychotic episodes, I listened with interest.

He said his story is published on a website which he referenced. He showed me his navy-blue cap he wears all the time, which encourages him when he feels down. On the front of the hat were the words **DON'T QUIT** in white and neon green letters for the **DO IT**. Around the lower curvature of the bill of the cap were the words PRAY & NEVER GIVE UP. On the white adjustable band in the back was the Scripture reference: "One day Jesus told his disciples a story to show that they should always pray and never give up" (Luke 18:1 [NLT]).

My check was for $12.76, but my bank records show I paid $122.76. Silvia got $100 and I gave $10 to Amber, the cashier who was so pleasant and told me about Silvia's personal financial needs. Both women hugged me. The one who received the $100 was crying.

Souvenir Extravaganza

For they refreshed my spirit and yours also. Such men deserve recognition.

—1 Cor. 16:18 THE HOLY BIBLE, NEW INTERNATIONAL VERSION® *(NIV)*

Tuesday, May 29

On Tuesday morning, I bought gifts and souvenirs before I left Fancy Gap. I'd picked them out the night before. I tried to convince myself that I wasn't really full-blown manic, though just in case, I'd slept on it before buying the gifts. All but one were sort of sensible—the hideous tee shirt I bought for Nicole, not so much. I won't even show it to her. The shirt was purple with metallic gold and pink letters, colors of the Advent in the Christian Church Year (roughly 40 days leading up to Christmas). These royalty colors represent the coming of King Jesus.

The back of the shirt is blank, but the front says, "My husband is a RICH man (Joshua 24:15). He has a strong faith, children who love him, and a wife who adores him." Below this is written:

COURAGEOUS: HONOR BEGINS AT HOME
But if you refuse to serve the Lord, then choose today whom you will serve. Would you prefer the gods your ancestors served beyond the Euphrates? Or will it be the gods of the Amorites in whose land you now live? But as for me and my family, we will serve the Lord (Joshua 24:15 ([NLT]).

Other gifts and souvenirs purchased were a 500-piece puzzle for Megan depicting important historical facts and places in Virginia; a beanie bag Dale Earnhardt car with key chain for my two-year-old grandson Ethan; a coffee cup with red cardinals for my ninety-seven-year-old aunt, which I broke before I could give to her; a gray sweatshirt too small for Elijah with three evergreens in the background of a large black bear (not to scale) that read *Fancy Gap Virginia*; an (also too small) tee shirt for Megan with butterflies and the words *Fancy Gap Virginia* (of course); three khaki baseball caps with a rail fence, some grass, and what looks like a 1942 pickup truck like the one we had on our farm growing up, all embossed in matching brown thread. I gave one to Alan for his brother Sam, and I still have two left. Elijah and my son-in-law, Richard, don't wear baseball caps, especially ones with *Fancy Gap*

VA on them. Megan thought it referred to a GAP knock-off department store. Who's heard of the town Fancy Gap!

The most desirable gifts I bought were three crystal clear rectangular prism paperweights ($8.99 each) with hologram statues of the Raising the Flag on Iwo Jima inside with the inscription: Washington, DC. At least they didn't attribute that one to Fancy Gap! I put one on Lora's desk by reaching through the small hole in the security window. I also left one at Alan's for his sister-in-law Cathy, and I kept one for myself. All together, I bought fourteen items that morning for a total of $116.97, an average of $8.30 per item.

The total cost for lodging, food, tips, gifts, and souvenirs was less than $500. But had I not gotten some rest, I don't think I would have been able to drive all the way home before the *Big One* episode took place. This $500 was a small price for a two-day breather. I brought home $117 in gifts and people were healed and blessed financially. I like to give things to people. It brings greater joy to give than to receive (Acts 20:35).

Home by the Skin of My Teeth

*Do not be afraid or discouraged, for the Lord will personally
go ahead of you. He will be with you; he will neither fail you
nor abandon you.*

—Deut. 31:8 (NLT)

Tuesday, May 29

Fancy Gap, VA to Pulaski, VA

May 29

I didn't have T-Mobile cell service inside my motel room, but I checked my voicemail before I left the Cochran Market and found a message from Alan saying, "You're this close; you might as well come visit me." When I'd called the night before, he'd said he was too sick to have company. I was not surprised. It always takes him a little time to become accustomed to change, including visitors invading his comfortable space. So I headed north on US Route 52 toward Pulaski, a distance of thirty-five miles away. The detour only added about forty minutes to my total trip home.

When I arrived, I knew I was a little manicky, so I consciously tried to not show it. I had no idea that it could turn into a full-blown psychotic manic episode. My friend Charles, a homeless man that I had met in February 2018 at a men's prayer breakfast, had pointed me to some Scriptures to confirm that my mind was healed. Isaiah 54:17 says no weapon that is formed against me shall prosper. I read in 2 Corinthians 5:17 that if I belong to Christ, I am a new person. The old life is gone; a new life has begun! 1 Corinthians 2:16 states that I have the mind of Christ. And Romans 8:37 declares I am more than a conqueror through Christ who loves me.

The first thing I wanted to show Alan was that I'd overcome my fear of cats (mostly). After the tragic death of my cat when I was a young child, I began having dreams that tiny black cats were crawling all over the floor in my bedroom and I couldn't get out of bed. I didn't tell Mom, but we didn't know anything about counseling back then, anyway. It would have just made me look stupid. Before 2015, I wouldn't sit down in a room with a cat; I was afraid it would attack me. I'd stand up and never take my eyes off my enemy cat.

My cousin Lois has a cat she's particularly fond of because it came to her house the day her husband died. She lives fifty miles away from my home in Knoxville. Once while driving to visit her, I told myself, 'If you can't spend the night there without having her put Cinder up, you have to stay in a motel." Since I couldn't really afford to do that at the time, I decided to buckle up and bite the bullet. I reasoned that even if Cinder did attack me, I probably wouldn't die. Ever since, I've been able to let a cat sit in my lap or lie in my bed with me without completely freaking out. It's still hard for me to pick up a cat though. They feel so bony!

I asked Alan to pick up his cat Rubbins and put him in my arms as if I were holding a baby. Feet facing upward, toward the ceiling. He stayed there for a few minutes, long enough for Alan to take some pictures, but then he jumped down. Recently, Alan told me that he knew I was manic. It was probably because of that stunt! But he wasn't worried about me jumping off the deep end, or he would have called my family. Actually, no one saw the breakdown coming!

I'd bought gifts at Cochran's store for Alan, his brother Sam, and sister-in-law Cathy. I left the Fancy Gap baseball cap and an Iwo Jima paperweight with Alan. The night before, I'd called Sam from Shoney's thanking him for his army service. I thought these were fitting gifts for Memorial Day. I was obviously confused. Sam was not even dead, so he couldn't have been killed in the line of duty!

Alan wouldn't accept any of the gifts I had purchased for him. He showered me with gifts, though. He had recently purchased the book *Josephus: The Complete Works* and had planned to mail it to me. He had given me lots of gifts in the past, but this was the first one since he moved to Pulaski in 2013. He also gave me *Lefty Frizzell: The Honky-tonk Life of Country Music's Greatest Singer* by Daniel Cooper, a friend of his. This was probably Alan's only copy, but he knows what a Lefty fan I am. He was so sexy and could sing a lick too! Alan rounded out his gift giving with two collections of videos: *Tracy & Hepburn: The Signature Collection* and *Classic Monsters: The Definitive Collection (Dracula, Frankenstein, The Wolf Man, Together Again for the First Time)*.

I used to get mad when Alan would criticize my gifts for him or would totally reject them and give them back. I now understand that Alan embodies the spirit of Jesus, who said, "It is more blessed to give than to receive." He really does enjoy giving people stuff.

Pulaski to Wytheville, VA

May 29

When I left Pulaski, it was beginning to sprinkle rain. After I'd traveled about twenty-five miles on I-81 S, I felt hungry again. The cookies Alan had given me hadn't done the trick. I found a Denny's in Wytheville. My bank records show I spent $166.87 there. Kind of expensive for a bowl of vegetable soup and a grilled cheese sandwich! But there's an explanation.

I had prayed for my server for healing of hearing and her back or leg pain (probably both), and she was healed. When she was in the back, another employee told me she worked harder than any of the other servers. She was a single mom working to take care of her family despite incredible pain. I had an idea. Denny's promotion at the time was Star Wars memorabilia. I bought one of every cup or trading card that they had to give to Richard for Christmas. I hadn't found anything suitable at Cochran's. I tipped 100% on the meal and the Star Wars souvenirs. I think that came to $66.87, and I rounded her tip up to $100.

Wytheville to Bristol, VA

May 29

It was seventy miles from Wytheville to Bristol, VA. I'd left the Lakeview Restaurant in Fancy Gap at 8:00 a.m. I spent time at Cochran's Store picking out souvenirs and talking with and praying for two older gentlemen with diabetes. I probably visited Alan for a couple of hours. And I spent some extra time at Denny's in Wytheville interacting with the servers. So it took me ten hours after leaving the Lakeview Restaurant to drive to Bristol, VA, a distance of about 135 highway miles.

It rained most of the way from Wytheville to Bristol, but as I neared Bristol, it was pouring down rain, and it became hard to see out my windshield. I was also very tired, so I got off the Interstate at Lee Highway to try to find a hotel or motel.

I surfed the Internet looking for cheap motels. I passed a few and rejected them because there were few or no cars. One of them was painted pink and had pink flamingo yard art. I was tempted to stay there, but there were only a couple of cars. This is also my usual criterion for choosing non-chain restaurants when I'm traveling. The Lakeview Restaurant and Mountain Top Motel in Fancy Gap had been exceptions. I'd been hungry, sleepy, tired, and desperate.

After driving a few miles on Lee Highway without seeing much civilization, just a farm equipment store and a few other businesses that couldn't help me, I finally found a Roadrunner gas and convenience store about 8 p.m. I went to the restroom and then paid for my gas and a Dunkin' Donuts iced mocha coffee drink. I'd found a coupon near the cooler case for the coffee. I couldn't use it, though, because the cashier was wearing very thick glasses and couldn't read the expiration date on the coupon, even by holding it close to his face with or without his glasses. The coffee was $2.76, and I tried to tip him $5, but he wouldn't accept it.

Outside, a man was sitting up against the wall of the building, beside his small motorcycle. I felt the Holy Spirit telling me to pray for him. I asked if he needed help.

He needed a jump start for his battery. He said he had asked a few young people for help, but they didn't help him. Maybe they didn't have cables, but his assessment was that young people didn't help so much anymore.

I had jumper cables, and he was happy to get it started. I asked him if he needed money. He said he could use some for his wife and him. He might have lost his job. Don't remember. But his wife and he were former drug addicts.

I told him about Todd White and his healing from drug and alcohol addictions. I didn't mention Todd's addiction to pornography since he was eleven years old.

The man had recently been talking with his uncle about going to church with him. He spoke fondly about his late grandmother and her godly influence. I probably gave him about $80 hidden in a diaper inside a pouch on the outside of my luggage. He didn't see where I got it. It was all I had that was easily accessible.

I went back inside the store to pray for the healing of the cashier's eyes. I felt the Holy Spirit leading me to do that. I asked him which of the motels on Lee Highway were safe. He said none of the ones close by were, but recommended a chain hotel farther down the road, maybe Holiday Inn or Comfort Inn. I've forgotten. This time I insisted strongly that he take a tip, and I laid a $5 bill on the counter.

I ended up turning the wrong way out of the parking lot and just got on the Interstate and drove the rest of the 125 miles home.

Bristol to Knoxville, TN

May 29

I was blessed that I didn't stay in Bristol that night. It was the next morning at my home that my psychotic manic episode became full blown. Had I stayed in Bristol, I might have gone naked in public and ended up in jail or a mental hospital. They might not have had a way to contact my family. I've since added that information to the medical information I always carry.

I got off I-40 W at Exit 398, Strawberry Plains Pike, to take a back way home. My friend Winnie had told me I wouldn't recognize the new entrance to my subdivision off Alcoa Highway. I imagined the construction had been completed a couple of years early and I wouldn't be able to navigate the new frontage road entrance. That would have been irrelevant, since I would be entering a back entrance to my subdivision.

I wanted to eat at the Cracker Barrel, where I usually eat when I come home this way, but it was 10:30 p.m. and therefore it was closed. Fortunately, the Krystal next door was open. I ordered something for $3.04 and paid for it with a $20 bill. There were three employees at the time, including Dana, the manager. I wanted to give each of them $5 of my change, but they wouldn't take it.

I tried to get a truck driver who was traveling to Charlotte to give them the $15, but he wouldn't take the money to give to them. It would be the same as if I did, but I didn't reason that one out. I asked if he was a Christian. He said yes.

I then asked him to go to a Jamaican restaurant near a Goodwill in North Charlotte and tell the couple who owned it about Jesus. I didn't remember the name of it, but I described the couple. I had felt like the man at the restaurant did voodoo or witchcraft on me; maybe that would explain the itchy rash I'd had the last few days I spent in Charlotte before going to Winston-Salem. The voodoo man had been very suspicious of me because I'd given a copy of the short bio I'd written about myself to his wife. She was very interested because her sister was in a nursing home, and she didn't think she should be there. The woman and I had carried on a friendly conversation. Her husband asked her gruffly how she knew me. He seemed to be angry when she told him she had just met me.

The truck driver was a nice man. He didn't say anything about that one. He didn't dine in, though. He made a bee line for his truck.

As I left, I told the Krystal employees that I had dropped $15 on the table where I ate. They could keep it or let the next patron find it. I was pushy. Once I'd decided to tip everywhere I ate, it became a mandate that I couldn't ignore.

Governor John Sevier Highway (SR 168) is a left-hand turn off Strawberry Plains Pike, four miles past the Krystal. I was okay through that intersection because there was a traffic light, but I didn't remember the name of the road I turned onto. I became disoriented at the split between Governor John Sevier Hwy and Chapman Highway on the left. I recognized a few things on Chapman that I could see near the fork, but I missed the turn and proceeded on the nameless road I was traveling. It appeared to me to run parallel to Chapman Highway, but it didn't.

I continued on SR 168 for about six miles, thinking I was going to "nowhere." The trees beside the road seemed eerie. Finally, I saw the Dollar Store where I was supposed to turn right. I didn't remember the five more turns during the remaining three miles home. The next thing I do remember seeing after the Dollar Store was the holly bushes in front of my house.

The holly bushes must've had dew or something on them. They looked to be frozen. I touched a branch to see if it was, and a briar lightly pricked my finger. I thought of it as a frozen hedge of protection to defend me from intruders. Maybe demons too, at that point. Also, as I got to my front door, I saw the heavy ivy in front of the house next to the porch. Since I erroneously believed there might be snakes in there, it would serve as a moat to protect me for the rest of the walkway in front of my house.

During that seemingly long drive home from Krystal, I kept thinking that Governor John Sevier Highway was somehow part of that new entrance to my subdivision. Later, as my psychotic manic episode continued, I worried that other people wouldn't recognize that new interchange either. It would seem like a new city to them. I imagined there would be interstate cloverleafs, six-lane highways, and so on.

This notion continued into my psychosis drama. The mount where President Trump, Hillary Clinton, and Benjamin Netanyahu would break the glass ceiling was located near that entrance to my subdivision, at the house where an episode of Oxygen TV's *Mark of a Killer* was filmed earlier in 2018.

Sometimes this new entrance contained a corner gate of the Garden of Eden. At times, it was the Temple Mount in Jerusalem. Sometimes it was one of the twelve gates in Heaven. And sometimes it was located at Megan's home in Charlotte or at the location of Covington Fellowship Church.

PART IV

FALLING DOWN THE RABBIT HOLE

Meemaw3

May 29–June 4, 2018

Manic Delusions in the Boudoir

And here's to the fools who dream
Crazy as they may seem
Here's to the hearts that break
Here's to the mess we make

—"Audition (The Fools Who Dream)" from *La La Land (2016)*
Lyrics by Benj Pasek and Justin Paul

Tuesday, May 29–Monday, June 4

Theme: Entering La La Land

Backstory

I arrived home about 11:30 p.m. on Tuesday, May 29 and collapsed into my bed. I slept well. I'd been exhausted. This was to be the only sleep I would get until I was taken by ambulance to the University General Hospital on June 4. It's not uncommon to go without sleep for several days during a psychotic manic episode, in my case, five nights.

I woke up late. Since I'd been out of town for more than six weeks, my cupboard was bare. For breakfast I ate two leftover Krystal Chiks. I also had a piece of a biscuit from the Lakeview Restaurant in Fancy Gap. This became the showbread in later scenes of my psychotic episode.

I thought this might be a good time to fast for a few days. I'd always wanted to fast but was afraid to because of my diabetes. I prayed and asked God if it was safe for me to fast now that I was completely healed of everything. Fasting turned out to not be optional, as my full-blown psychotic episode became increasingly *full blown.* I never get hungry or sleepy during one of these episodes.

After breakfast, I brought in my four pieces of luggage, the gifts I'd bought in Fancy Gap and Wytheville, my shoes, two large plastic bags of dirty laundry, and a host of phones, tablets, and laptops.

Sometime Wednesday afternoon Leslie and her teenage daughter Sherry came to visit, presumably to check on me. Their apartment had flooded, and they were living with my friends Rick and Judy, who live across the street, until they could find a place to live. I'd never met the pair, though I'd seen Leslie in the hallway sometimes when I came over to pick up or give something to Rick or Judy. I'd been moderately manic, just shy of psychotic, earlier that morning when I'd dropped in to see my neighbors.

I'd placed a black, simulated leather portfolio binder containing a legal-sized notepad in the middle of my kitchen table. At my request, they signed their names with Leslie's email address on the first page. Later, I was to think of it as an earthly record book with the names of new converts to submit to Jesus for the real Lamb's Book of Life.

Beside the black binder was a large, cinnamon-scented candle inside a jar and the handheld butane stick lighter I'd used to light it. I thought of it as an Eternal Flame, which I burned during the duration of my psychotic manic episode at home. That concept might have been triggered in my mind by the Eternal Flame at John F. Kennedy's grave, though it would've fit the themes of my psychosis better if I'd thought of it as a *Ner Tamid* sanctuary lamp representing the menorah of the Temple in Jerusalem. I'd only recently learned of the Hanukkah Miracle. They only had enough oil to keep the Temple's menorah burning for one day, but miraculously, it lasted eight days.

When I'm manic, I can hide it for maybe thirty minutes to an hour if I don't want a psychiatrist or other professional, or a friend or family member to figure it out. I used to dress up and wear lipstick and other makeup for my psychiatrist appointments. Since I rarely wear either, it was a foolproof way to stay out of the hospital, at least for a while.

Leslie is an LCSW mental health counselor in private practice. In this case, it helped that my house hadn't been ransacked yet and I had acted *normal*, so she wasn't alerted or alarmed. She didn't visit me again until Monday, June 4, after my neighbors became alarmed that they hadn't seen me for a few days and Rick found me naked on the floor of my den.

Setting

My illness degenerated at a fast pace from this point onward. I stripped my bed of its sheets, probably intending to do laundry, but that never happened. I retrieved some of my treasure boxes on the top shelf of a closet in my bedroom and put them on the bare bed.

The treasures included family Bibles that had belonged to Dad, who passed away in 1959, and Mammaw, Mother's mom, who died in 1983, right before Megan was born. Only Dad's was an authentic Family Bible with a Family Registry. In olden times, Family Bibles were used to verify births, deaths, and marriages in the absence of birth, marriage, or death certificates. It's interesting to me that my parents' names, their birthdates, and date of marriage were in Mom's handwriting, their three children's names and birth dates were in Dad's, and I had recorded the deaths of each of my parents.

Two boxes contained baby clothes that had been worn by Megan or Elijah—a girl box and a boy box. Another box had the stuffed animals that had played significant roles in my last full-blown psychotic episode in 1995. That episode had ended in the master bedroom, whereas this one resumed there after I returned home from Fancy Gap.

When the police had broken into my house in 1995, they'd found me in my bedroom, wearing only a leopard-skin camisole onesie bodysuit and reading my dad's Bible. I had completely gutted the room. All of my clothes had been moved to the hall or the living room and piled on the floor. The bedroom had been completely cleaned out to make a spaceship for my boyfriend, my two children, and me to *blast off to another planet* and start a new colony and civilization. In 1995, the only things left in the room, besides the empty furniture, had been the four stuffed animals that were named for each of us, a guitar, and my dad's Bible.

This 2018 episode would have a *blast off to other worlds* theme later in the week.

I also brought down a beautiful baby doll rocker bed that Daddy made for me when I was about four years old. I think it had been a crafts project for him in the Veteran's hospital during a mental breakdown. The base was of three-inch-thick solid oak wood, stained blonde to match the woven half-canopy basket where the baby doll lay. I fondly remember the two Tiny Tears dolls and their onesies, one trimmed in blue and the other with pink.

All but one of the suitcases was unopened and parked in front of the chest of drawers. The large pullman had been unzipped and was lying on the foot of the bed. Also on the bed were the gifts from Fancy Gap and most of the books I keep in the armoire on the left side of my bed. I have many other books in five other bookcases in my house, but most of the ones used as props in my episodic scenes came from this armoire. The drawers of this side cabinet held stacks of pictures of my children and grandchildren and the artwork they had made.

On Wednesday afternoon, May 30, I spent a few hours in the bedroom going through my children's boxes of clothing and looking for props in my two clothes closets. I didn't trash the closets or drawers in this 2018 full-blown manic episode like I had in 1995. The peculiarity of the layout this time was the makeup of the collections of articles on the bed, the Fancy Gap chicken sitting on top of the chest, and the items of clothing I retrieved from the closets and boxes.

Throughout the week, I was in and out of this room, acting out vignettes with themes and variations, or selecting props for scenes in other parts of the house. Since the timeline was not linear, the easiest way to explain what happened is to use the format of *levels* of a video game that can be played over and over without any specified order of play.

Level 1: Baby Dedication

The main point of this vignette was to present Megan to her husband, Richard, as a suitable wife (they had been married for almost seven years) and to prepare for a big celebration of the birth of their only child, Calypso (who had been born over a year earlier). The baby celebration was to be held at Covington Fellowship Church in Charlotte, near where they live. My idea for the celebrations was inspired by the wedding of the daughter of the founders of the TTTV Christian TV network, which was covered for months on TTTV, leading up to the April 2018 wedding. Everything from how they met, the proposal, the bridal shower, and later the ceremony was documented on TTTV. It appeared to me to be as important as any royal wedding!

The dresser in the master bedroom became the focal point for this psychotic scene. I put a *baby cake* on the left side of the dresser top. This consisted of two receiving blankets, two baby towels, and some washcloths neatly wrapped in the shape of a round cake and held together by four large diaper pins. Thick baby socks were used to make candles. One was tacked to the cake with a pink bow using a straight pin, and a blue one was mirrored on the other side. It was a baby shower gift for Megan that I had kept for almost thirty-five years. I never took it apart.

Beside the cake, I put a framed wedding picture of Richard and Megan with Calypso's birth announcement photo leaning against the frame. On a beveled, five-inch oval mirror with the etching, *I Love You Always*, I placed a golden lapel pin formed with the words *Trust God*. My children had given me the mirror when they were young. The pin was a gift from my church for my birthday.

The two family Bibles were in the middle of the dresser in front of a picture I had painted depicting the serious multi-car pileup averted by angels in September 2015. In the upper right corner, I painted a rainbow reminiscent of Mahalia Jackson's rendition of "God Put a Rainbow in the Sky." At the bottom was written the verse: "God is our refuge and strength, always ready to help in times of trouble" (Ps. 46:1 [NLT]).

On the right side of the dresser, I put one of the fancy boxes the Iwo Jima paperweights I'd purchased in Fancy Gap came in. The box was almost as valuable as its contents. It was made of dark-blue, stiff cardboard with an imperceptible magnetic closure. The inside was lined with a royal blue silky fabric, and the top had a silver embossed Great Seal of the United States.

In the beginning of my psychotic episode, the far right-hand side of the dresser had a Ben and Candy Carson theme, but it would change upon subsequent trips to the bedroom. The box was open and contained a five-inch by two-inch *I'm With Ben* decal and some stickers with stylized people holding hands with simply the word *Ben* in cursive.

I'd always been an Independent, not belonging to any political party, so I'd been surprised when Candy contacted me by email asking me to send a note of encouragement to Ben before the first Republican primary debate in 2015. I did. I don't know how she got my name and email address, since I'd only donated $25 at that point to his campaign. I believe it was supernatural, since it directly led to my assumed healing from bipolar disorder. I believed I really was healed, and this 2018 episode was an anomaly precipitated by a preventable set of circumstances.

In front of the Carson Box, I placed the stuffed dog toy that I chose to represent my new, soon-to-be-born, one-year-old grandbaby. The dog is light brown with a white belly and mangled tail. I moved the multicolored ceramic chicken statue here from the top of the chest and spruced it up with a Ben Carson hat, of course. Occasionally, I would change the hat to a Fancy Gap hat or a Calvin Klein, or all three simultaneously. Additionally, in front of the chicken, I placed two books and a CD:

> *My Life* by Ben Carson, MD with Cecil Murphy (based on the book *Gifted Hands*)

> *A Doctor in the House: My Life with Ben Carson* by Candy Carson

> *A VERY CANDY Christmas CD FEATURING CANDY CARSON With Special Guests*
> *Ricky Skaggs, Tony Orlando, Jason Crabb, AND MANY MORE!*

On the bed, I prepared a dowry for the new baby. I put the smaller items in the baby doll cradle my father had made for me. I lined it with a soft, loosely woven yellow baby receiving blanket with matching fringe. I added a pink baby sunsuit with yellow ducks and three rows of ruffles of the same material on the back bottom. My mom had made it for me in the early 1950s. There was also a linen, navy-blue dress, size 2T, with a white collar edged with two rows of tatting lace. A red satin ribbon bow with long streamers was attached with a medium-sized safety pin.

Other contents of the doll cradle were the thirty-five-year-old pink plastic squeeze toy doll given to Megan when she was a newborn, which was to survive the toy purge in another game. Also, there was a lei with cloth flowers and a coin purse purchased in Hawaii on one of the vacations with my kids. The only featured money for this video game world level was a $5 bill I placed in the doll cradle inside one of my two copies of the *My Life* by Ben Carson book.

My Russian friend Katya had given me a set of matryoshka wooden nesting dolls, which I included to stimulate the new baby's mental reasoning. She even came with an owner's manual: *Children Learn What They Live: Parenting to Inspire Values* by Dorothy Law Nolte and Rachel Harris. I put the book next to the baby cake, along with Mom's antique drawstring purse, which was to be used as a diaper bag. The purse/diaper bag was weaved in potholder style with pastel shades of pink, beige, blue, and white loops.

In future visits to the master bedroom, I would present to Richard clothes the baby would need when she got older. Specifically, I gave him Megan's shiny white baptismal dress, which my mother and I had made for her water baptism when she was ten years old. There was also an aqua, nylon chiffon bridesmaid's dress and Megan's gown and mortarboard from her doctoral graduation.

Level 2: Visited by an Angel-o

On Friday, June 1, there was a knock at the door. I peeped out of an adjacent window. I'd never seen the guy before, but I invited him inside, anyway. He was a young, twenty-something Latino who looked nonthreatening. In my delusion, I imagined him to be Todd White's associate, who would carry on the mission as a Lifestyle Christian. In particular, he would go to Canada, where Todd White has been banned.

Angelo told me he represented AT&T. I told him I didn't trust them, briefly explaining my hacking experiences during 2017. He said he represented other companies too. So I reasoned he was okay.

I told him about his mission. I showed him my Canada snow globe as proof. He smiled in agreement. I invited him to follow me into the totally ransacked part of my house. The floors of the toy room, master bath, and hallway were strewn with toys, books, and stuffed animals from playing the Toy Room Story *Luck of the Landing* game (described in another psychotic vignette), but we were able to climb over stuff to get to the master bedroom, where there were items I wanted him to take on his journey.

My friend Rachel is an accomplished American author and filmmaker. I had some of her books, but I gave Angelo my three favorites to help him find Rachel at her home in New York. Two were signed copies.

I even gave him an autographed copy of my all-time favorite novel. It had been an official Book-of-the-Month Club selection in 1990. I bought a used copy, and Rachel signed it for me one year at a Human Genome

Conference in Hilton Head, SC where my biotech software company always exhibited. I gave him an unsigned copy of one of her less successful recent novels.

In 2011, Rachel had somehow found out the address of the rehab center where I was recovering from a broken hip and sent me one of her racy novels, which she signed, "To my friend Ruth, who is in between boyfriends."

I remarked to Angelo that the cover of that one was a bit risqué—a woman wearing a sexy red teddy with a black garter belt and black stilettos heightened the intrigue. I told him I'd kept it in a drawer at the rehab center because I didn't want the nurses to think I was reading a *dirty* book. I added that the book was erotic, but well written. I had to tell him who John Updike was, but I explained it was a big deal to have his endorsement on the cover.

I felt a little dirty myself. Like a "Mrs. Robinson" or something. But unlike other psychotic manic episodes, I had no intentions of trying to seduce Angelo or anyone else. As he walked back to the living room, I stopped by the Toy Room to get a brand-new Jewish prayer shawl (tallit gadol) for him to take to Rachel. I explained that she is of Jewish ethnicity, but I was not aware whether she practices Judaism. I asked him to stop by her house on his way to Canada and present the Gospel to her and tell her we are definitely living in the End Times.

I've been burdened with Rachel's soul ever since I sent her a Christmas story I'd written in the early 2000s called "The Surprise Gift." It was about my mother crocheting afghans for all of us, including grandchildren and in-laws, with crippled rheumatoid arthritic hands. Every year she would give us money, but she always had something else, which she called the *surprise gift*. I concluded my story with the parallel that Jesus' first coming was also a Surprise Gift 2000 years ago. Rachel said the first part of the story was well written, but the last part was distracting, or something that let me know she thought I should have stopped before the part about Jesus.

I ushered Angelo to the door, but before I let him go, I completely changed the plan. I decided to transfer the charge to visit Rachel and go to Canada from Angelo to Brad, a young guy who worked at the T-Mobile store in Chapman Square. I explained that I'd recently purchased a tee shirt from his new side business. Angelo was to convey all the stuff I'd given him and to explain the game plan for stopping by Rachel's house on the way to his Canadian mission field.

In later chapters, I chronicle my stay at Broadmoor Regional Hospital for psychiatric treatment of my psychosis. After I returned from Broadmoor, I went to T-Mobile in Chapman Square. They told me Brad worked for Sprint now. They said no one had come in with books or anything to give to him. I called Brad, and he told me no one had given him anything either. I contacted AT&T a few times, and they just indicated how absurd it was to ask if they knew of a subcontractor that might have sent someone to my house during that time frame. It was like looking for a needle in a haystack!

I console myself by saying those items were idols of sorts—worshiping Rachel as a writer—and if my house had burned down in a later psychotic saga in my den, which was a real possibility, I wouldn't have the books and prayer shawl, anyway.

Level 3: Potty Training

No dowry for a parent and child would be complete without instructions for potty training, a significant milestone in the life of a toddler. This warrants its own scene in the Boudoir. I got the idea for this part of the saga from the *I Can Do It!* potty chart in the stack of memorabilia, drawings, and pictures of my grandchildren, which I found in one of the armoire drawers.

This chart reminded me of the two books Megan had bought for me one Christmas as a joke. So I included them in this scene.

> *What's Your Poo Telling You?* and *Poo Log—A Record Keeper,* both by Josh Richman and Anish Sheth, MD, Illustrations by Peter Arkle

Poo (not Pooh) and I have had a longstanding relationship. I've always been obsessed with pooping. It probably started with Mom giving me enemas several times per week. She was obsessed with regularity. I always look at my poop before flushing. Once, during a routine visit to my psychiatrist, I found one that looked like a guppy. I named him Bubba. I told my psychiatrist about it after he called me back to his office. His solution was to not look at my poo anymore. But that obsessive addiction was too difficult to break.

In times of extreme (non-psychotic) mania, I sometimes imagined I had worms in my poop. A few times in the early to mid-2000s, I thought my intestines had worms. One time in this period, I collected some samples in separate baggies, which I kept in a red plastic Folgers coffee can. Sometime during one of these severe manic times, I took my Folgers can to my gastroenterologist's office, but the nurse insisted they didn't need it. It smelled putrid!

Another time, after my Coronary Artery Bypass Graft (CABG) heart surgery in 2009, I had chest pains and drove myself to the Emergency Room. The home fecal worm kit I had requested earlier showed I didn't have worms, but I didn't take no for an answer. I called my roommate Alan and asked him to bring my Folgers can. He didn't know its contents. I gave the can to my orderly for an analysis. When he came back, he said the analysis showed no worms. I doubt if they tested it. The stench was beyond reeking.

I asked for the can back, but he had discarded it. I became upset, so he reluctantly retrieved it. He didn't appear too happy when he came back with it. When I texted Elijah about it, autocorrect changed it to a *gopher can*.

He asked for clarification.

Toy Room Story

We're going into attic mode, folks. Keep your accessories with you at all times. Spare parts, batteries, anything you need for an orderly transition.

—Buzz Lightyear, *Toy Story 3*

Tuesday, May 29–Monday, June 4
Theme: Luck of the Landing Game

Backstory

In 2013, I turned my guest bedroom into a child's room for my grandchildren. At that time, my grandchildren were two years old and a newbie. At the time of this 2018 psychotic manic episode, my grandchildren were ages one, two, five, and almost seven. All children who visited my house made a beeline for the Toy Room.

This room has a queen-sized bed covered by a colorful quilt with appliques of high heel shoes. My grandson, Ethan, is not old enough to care. Two cherry-finish wooden hutch-style desks, each with three drawers, a desktop, and two shelves are on the front wall, and a matching chest of drawers is located on the back wall.

The chest of drawers sits beside the entrance to the closet. A handmade canopy doll bed sits atop the chest. The canopy is pink with little bear prints and tatted white lace edging. A fancy bear with a full, flowing floral-print dress with an outer layer of gathered beige lace lies leisurely on the bed, wearing pearl beads and earrings.

Hanging on the front of the chest is a plaque with a picture of a young girl with golden curls. She's wearing a white flannel nightgown and kneeling on a cord rug, with clasped praying hands reaching up toward heaven. The inscription at the bottom is the traditional children's bedtime prayer: *Now I lay me down to sleep, I pray the Lord my soul to keep.*

The closet is no longer functional for holding clothes. I removed the clothes rod and added removable wire shelving to make more room to hold toys. The shelves are filled with books, pull toys, puzzles, art supplies, a toy cash register, pianos, guitars, microphones, and a large adult exercise ball, to name a few of the items. I removed the sliding doors and initially covered the closet opening with Minnie Mouse curtains, but now that I have a grandson, I've changed it to a shower curtain with a celestial motif of sun, moon, and stars.

The desks are filled with books and toys. Among them are my Little Golden Books from childhood: *The Little Red Hen, Little Red Riding Hood,* and *Rootie Kazootie Detective.* In addition to classics like *The Three Little Pigs* and *The Foot Book* by Dr. Seuss, I haven't forgotten their Christian learning with books like *The Picture Bible* (Endorsed by Protestants and Catholics, Appeals to all ages) and *The Illustrated Bible for Children.*

Two antique cedar chests that belonged to my mother and one of her sisters face each other on the other opposing walls. I removed the lids from them for safety reasons and filled them with toys—dolls and stuffed animals in the one with the original cedar finish and miscellaneous stuff like balls, barns, and dollhouses in the one that had been découpaged in pewter green to fit the color scheme of my brother's room. Originally these toy boxes were filled with toys that had mostly belonged to Megan, but I added many more from Goodwill and other thrift stores.

No Toy Room would be complete without my child-size rocking chair and the wooden high chair beside the door that Mom had used when I was a baby. One of my brothers had refinished them with a walnut stain to match. The antique chair has a toddler-size Mrs. Claus doll sitting in it. The room also sports a spring-based rocking horse and a folding table with three chairs, a Goodwill purchase (which explains the odd number of chairs).

I always decorate the room according to the season—Christmas, Valentine's Day, St. Patrick's Day, Easter, and others. At the time of this severe manic psychotic episode, there were plenty of bunnies, chickens, and ducks, some sitting (or imaginary setting) on plastic eggs in a beautiful, natural wood basket.

Game Description

During this part of my psychotic episode, I imagined that some of my toys were not safe or suitable for some of my grandchildren. Some were just plain unacceptable for any of them! I planned to ask Nicole, the mother of three of the children, to help me sort the toys.

I did a pre-sort for her in a lottery fashion as a board game with levels, as if in a video game. I call this game *Luck of the Landing.* I suspect it was motivated by Jesus' parable of the sower and the seed (Mark 4:1-20).

I later came home from Broadmoor to find the Toy Room turned upside down. Toys, books, and stuffed animals were strewn on the bed, all over the floor, some in the hallway, some in cardboard boxes, and even some in the hall bathroom.

Setup

The format for the game layout is as follows. Four medium-size cardboard boxes are placed on the floor—one inside the Toy Room (*Heaven*), one in the doorway (*Purgatory*), another in the hall outside the Toy Room (*Get Out of Jail Free*), and one in the hall bathroom (*Hell*). The toys and books in the Toy Room were the game pieces for this board/video game.

Playing Instructions

First, I would select a game piece from somewhere in the Toy Room. If I knew it was a definite keeper, I would put it in the *Heaven* box, or super-special keepers were placed on the bed. If I felt strongly that a toy should not be kept, I put it in the *Hell* box in the bathroom.

If a game piece was not predetermined to be in *Heaven* or *Hell*, I would stand near the back wall of the Toy Room and throw the toy or book to see where it landed. Anything that landed on the floor surrounding a box or was hanging on the box edge was left for Nicole to decide the outcome.

Any thrown game piece that landed inside the *Heaven* box was an automatic keeper. If a game piece landed inside *Purgatory*, Nicole could decide if it was a keeper (*Heaven*), a giveaway (*Get Out of Jail Free*), or a throwaway (*Hell*). As a Protestant Christian, I don't believe in Purgatory, but what the heck! It's only a game!

A toy or book in the *Purgatory* box was not suitable, but didn't need punishment and a cleansing like the ones who went to the *Hell* box. If I threw a game piece past *Purgatory* and it landed inside the *Get Out of Jail Free* box, it would definitely be given away, maybe to Goodwill. This saved-by-the bell box has no counterpart in Protestant or Catholic theology.

The game pieces I physically placed in the *Hell* box were supposed to have first been tortured in my walk-in handicap shower. The water comes out so forcefully that Megan calls it a torture chamber. Those game pieces in *Hell* were particularly hideous or offensive and must be removed from the house. I don't recall actually putting any of the toys and books in the shower, though. To avoid further contamination, I would later put most of these despicable ones in a huge black, plastic leaf bag which I put outside on my front porch.

Game Play

I entered this room multiple times to play the game on separate levels as the psychotic episode progressed. I began randomly picking out things from the toy chests, hutch desks, and the closet for my pre-sort.

I first chose the items with sentimental value and either put them on the bed or threw them in the *Heaven* box on the floor of the Toy Room. I kept the pink plastic doll squeeze toy that my cousin Peggy had given Megan when she was born. And of course I had to save the blue seersucker bunny, mallard ducks, and blue geese stuffed toys Mom had made for Megan and Elijah to play with. The royal blue stuffed bear with red hearts all over it that I made during my nesting instinct before Megan was born was definitely a keeper. I'd used the same cloth material to make the matching window shades, wall hangings with clowns and stuffed balloons, diaper stacker, and crib bumper pads for the nursery. I kept my childhood Little Golden Books and the Bible storybooks for the grandchildren.

I threw the toys and books that were obviously unsuitable for all the children into the box in the bathroom. Anything that said, "Warning: Choking Hazard," had to go. The SLIME was made in China. Who knew what ingredients were in that stuff! Maybe lead or other poisonous substances? Both boxes of slime needed to go!

Why was Po, the potty-mouthed Teletubby, left in the Toy Room in the first place? I knew that when her tummy was pressed, she sometimes said something that sounded like, "F-g--t, f-g--t! F-g--t, f-g--t! F-g--t! F-g--t! Bite my butt!" The toy company that made those insisted that the Cantonese woman's voice was saying, "faster, faster" and "slower, slower." I think the next batch released after the controversy fixed Po's homophobic potty mouth. Ironically, an internet search gives links indicating that the woman behind Po's voice moved on to being in lesbian porn movies. I'm not sure if it's true, but it makes an interesting twist.

Of course Po should go from the Toy Room. It was even recalled and removed from the store shelves in the 90s. Since it's a collectors' item, I reasoned it should be kept somewhere out of the reach of the children. I ignored any pretense of spiritual discernment and kept it on the bed for now.

I put the three Furbies and Mr. Bigglesworth, Dr. Evil's hairless pet cat in the Austin Powers movies, into the *Hell* box in the bathroom. Sometimes in the middle of the night they would start making creepy noises and wake me up. It didn't dawn on me to remove the batteries. These toys definitely needed a cleansing in my walk-in torture chamber.

I also found a red, stuffed devil, complete with black horns and a red tail with a silky black triangular tip. It was holding a silk cylindrical pillow with lace on each end, bearing the misspelled inscription "Your [*sic*] as Sweet as They Come." It was made in Hong Kong by the Fukei Industrial Company.

I have no clue where that Valentine's Day toy came from! I know it wasn't Megan's or Elijah's or in any of the bags of toys my close friend Betty had given me for my grandchildren. Would I have purchased it at a Goodwill? Surely not. Heaven forbid!

The devil (satan) has no physical body of his own. The representation as a figure with a red suit, horns, and a pointy tail, usually holding a pitchfork instead of a pillow, has evolved over the centuries with roots in ancient mythology. This incarnation representation is not Biblical. He's an evil spirit who can only be in one place at a given time. One of the other fallen angels (demons) usually does his bidding. They can possess an animal or a human. This toy was so evil I took it to the front porch and put it in the large black leaf bag, skipping the cleansing process to quickly bypass further defilement of my house.

Drama on an Outdoor Stage

Your mind is a movie, your eyes are the projector, so everything you see is coming from you—me, her, him, the train, everything, everyone. But not only are you watching this movie, so is everyone else. And to top it off, you're starring in it and so is everyone else.

— L.A. Golding, *Lerkus: A Journey to End All Suffering*

Wednesday, May 30–Friday, June 1

Theme: A Beautiful Day in the Neighborhood

Backstory

It had begun raining hard in Bristol, VA on Tuesday evening, and persisted most of the way home, a distance of about 125 miles. I'd been totally out of it for the last twenty-five miles. My guardian angels had to work overtime!

The rain continued into much of the next day. It was warm and sunny most of the rest of that week, so I spent quite a bit of time outside. This was unusual for me. Surely neighbors, dog walkers, joggers, and other passersby noticed the peculiarity.

My car stayed in my driveway, and I left my yard only twice—once to tell my neighbors Rick and Judy that I'd returned home, and one time to place two coffee cups in the tan wooden porch swing that's on the side porch of Mrs. Walker's house across the side street.

In this drama, I will describe some of the things that happened during my episode that related to my yard or other houses in my neighborhood. It's fitting to string together some arbitrary scenes that don't conform to time or logical thematic development. However, these random thoughts do illustrate what goes on in a psychotic, manic brain.

Scene 1: Announcement of My Arrival

Wednesday, May 30

I'd been gone from my home for a month and a half, so I wanted to tell Rick and Judy, "I'm back!" I was experiencing severe mania at that time. Rick opened the door and invited me in. Leslie, the mental health counselor who was living with them, came to the door behind him.

I rudely barged past Rick and Leslie and went straight to Judy, who was standing back a few feet in the dining room. I put my hand on her shoulder and declared healing in Jesus' name for any members of her family that needed to be healed of mental illness.

If a *normal* person had done that, it would have been obvious that they should call my family to tell them I was having mental problems. But I used to go over there sometimes, almost as manic, to show Rick my phone during my days of cyber paranoia. "Look what the hackers did THIS time!" My baseline mood can be so weird, it's tough (even for doctors) to distinguish when I'm sick or just "Ruth being Ruth!"

Scene 2: The Good Samaritan

May 30

The man at the convenience store in Bristol, VA, who'd needed battery jumper cables, had said he'd asked everyone who came to the store if they'd help him jump start his motorcycle. None of them had wanted to help. He'd told me, "Young people just live for themselves these days!" He might not have been familiar with the term *millennials*.

So I decided to set up a relief/help station on the charcoal grill on my carport for anyone passing by my house who needed jumper cables, water, hand tools (hammer, wrenches, screwdrivers, tire gauges, etc.), garbage bags, or paper towels. I put these on the grill shelf along with the emergency kit I carry in my car with *everything* a motorist might ever need, except for a battery or spare tire. I left a note on my trash can telling people I had prepared this array of stuff to help people in need.

After a couple of days in the sun, I brought the gallon plastic container of water back into the house. I didn't want anyone to drink it and be harmed by phthalates. Phthalates have been shown to cause reproductive birth defects in male laboratory animals, and I didn't want to risk a thirsty boy mouse coming around here!

Scene 3: Thanking the Garbage Men

Thursday, May 31

Thursday is trash pickup day at my house. I wanted to reward my sanitation workers for doing such a great job, so I made a packet for them and placed it on top of the trash can. Since it had rained most of Wednesday, I put all of their gifts inside a clear plastic bag containing an 11" x 18" American flag window decal. The decal was made of perforated vinyl that was designed to keep the sun out. The mounting directions indicated the flag was suitable for the back windshield of a car or a home or office window. It also said, "Show Your Pride."

Among the other gifts I included were an Easy-to-Read Version (ERV) Bible with a $20 bill inside, marking John 3:16. On the back of the directions for the flag, I had written this note and placed it facing upward atop the gifts:

> Thank you for your service. I disposed of my own trash this week so you can have more time to enjoy the gift Jesus gave you [for free]. A priceless gift!! He <u>died</u> for your sins and mine. Also for any sicknesses. Claim your free gift at the foot of the cross.

I dragged the trash receptacle to the road next to my driveway, probably after they'd picked up the trash early that morning. It stayed there until sometime after I was taken to the University General Hospital on Monday, June 4. When I returned home on June 18, after a stay at Broadmoor Hospital, someone (probably Rick) had brought the trash can down to my house. Everything was on the top just as I had left it. I doubt if the sanitation workers ever saw the note or the goodies.

I do remember taking the trash can back to the end of my driveway the first Thursday after I returned from Broadmoor. I think I glanced in it and saw a bag of trash, but it didn't dawn on me to look inside to see if I had discarded something of sentimental or monetary value. There are pictures that are unaccounted for, but had my house burned to the ground (a real possibility), they (and maybe me) would probably be gone, anyway.

Scene 4: God Bless the Mailmen

Friday, June 1–Saturday, June 2

Early Friday morning, I put a $20 bill in an envelope with a note thanking my mail carrier for his service. I was outside the next day when my mail was delivered. I asked the mailman if he got my note and the money the day before. He said he didn't carry the mail that day; his sub-carrier must have taken it. I didn't have $20 with me at the time, but I told him I would give him something more valuable than the $20 later. I don't remember whether I was referring to an Easy-to-Read Version (ERV) Bible with $20, or that I would share the Gospel of Salvation with him sometime.

Scene 5: Social Butterfly

Wednesday, May 30–Saturday, June 2

I interacted with many passersby while standing at the road at the end of my driveway. I usually greeted them, and if they stopped to talk, I would chat a minute and then maybe invite them to meet me at Covington Fellowship Church in Charlotte for the celebration of the birth of my new granddaughter, Calypso. Never mind that she was over a year old.

Or I might invite them to the opening of the US Israel Embassy in Jerusalem. That was old news, too. That celebration had already happened on May 14, 2018. Remember, I was nuts; don't confuse me with the facts. The devil's in the details!

Or I might have invited them to a dedication ceremony for the Third Temple, which is predicted in End Times Prophecy to be constructed at the Temple Mount, the location of two former Jewish temples. The First Temple was built in 957 BC by King Solomon, son of King David, and was destroyed when Jerusalem was torched by the Babylonians in 587/586 BC. The Second Temple was reconstructed in 516 BC under the support of Zerubbabel, governor of the Persian province of Judah, and the grandson of Jehoiachin, King of Judah. The Second Temple was destroyed by the Roman Empire in 70 AD.

I gave no specific dates to the passersby for any of these three events, and since I had no takers, that wasn't important.

Scene 6: Meemaw Meets Mary

Thursday, May 31

The two people in my neighborhood I interacted with the most were Mary and Beryl.

Mary was a young brunette with long hair, which she usually pulled back in a ponytail. One day she was wearing a navy-blue T-shirt with the writing: **"MY PASSWORD IS THE LAST 8 DIGITS OF π."** I laughed, and she said I was the only person in the neighborhood that "got it." She is a structural engineer, a subspecialty of civil engineering. It's good to know that I hadn't forgotten all of my math knowledge during my severe manic episode. I knew that pi (π) is an irrational number that cannot be written as a fraction, and thus never repeats.

I bent over and told Mary's big white Chow Chow, Maylee, that she was welcome to poop in my yard or hide it in my Hosta flower bed anytime she wanted to. Mary said that would not be necessary. She is one of the few in my neighborhood who carries pooper scooper baggies. Just like in New York City!

I don't remember the stuff I told most people who passed by, but I do remember asking Mary to tell Jim Rouse something about his part in the End Times. He lived near the apex of my subdivision, right across from the house where an Oxygen TV episode had been filmed earlier in 2018. This was what gave me the idea of making commercials of my own during another part of my severe manic episode. I think at this time I was imagining that this vertex was the location of the "Temple Mount," where President Donald Trump and Hillary Clinton would go hand in hand to dedicate the Third Temple to be built in Jerusalem.

Sometimes my subdivision was Eden, sometimes Heaven, sometimes Jerusalem, and sometimes Charlotte, depending on the "story" I was living at the time. I think I gave Mary something to give to Jim that had to do with the End Times or one of the three dedications. Maybe I just told her to ask him to bring back the information I had loaned him about the Rouse family genealogy. Jim and I are distantly related.

Scene 7: Beryl, Our Formal Introduction

Thursday, May 31–Friday, June 1

Beryl is a slight-framed, sixty-something man whose build just blends in with the bicycle that he rides through the neighborhood regularly when he isn't mowing yards, weeding flower beds, or doing some other odd jobs for my neighbors. I've lived in my neighborhood for 28 years, and he's been around for 20 of them. I never knew his name until this psychotic breakdown.

I'd wave to Beryl sometimes when I was walking, jogging, or just driving by a yard he was mowing or weeding. He'd turn off the mower and mumble something softly that was unintelligible to me, and I'd just smile and reply with something like, "Have a great day!" He probably thought I was deaf, standoffish, or snooty. He'd be partially correct!

After I returned home from Broadmoor Hospital, Beryl and I talked at length one day while he was changing some light bulbs for me. I found out that he lives next door in Mrs. Walker's basement. I had suspected he lived there because his bicycle was often on her porch.

Beryl said he's boarded with a few other elderly women, and he finds another one when she dies. I found out that he knows practically everyone in the subdivision and bunches of stuff about them. He seems to be a bit inquisitive and eager to pass on information.

On Thursday morning, May 31, he rode his bicycle past my driveway. During this phase of my episode, I thought I was living in the Garden of

Eden, so when he complimented my beautiful yard, I just replied, "You know who my gardener is, don't you?" I'm sure he was thinking of Justin, who mows my yard. How would he have known I meant Jesus? Or that my yard was in Eden?

When he cruised past me again on Thursday afternoon, we exchanged names, and I said something like Beryl was the name of one of my uncles and made some reference to "Burl and Ives." He smiled, as if I was not the first to associate his name with Burl. He probably thought I'd said Burl Ives, but I'd confused the singer and actor with the printmaking firm named for its owners Currier and Ives. I wrote *Burl and Ives* next to Beryl's name when I put it in the Book of Life I was keeping in my kitchen.

Late that evening, before sunset, Beryl cycled around again, as he was accustomed to doing. When he passed by my Eden, a big storm was about to come. Thunder! Lightning! He was bicycling fast. I tried to reach him to stop him with my hands. I think he either wanted to take cover for himself or he wanted to calm Mrs. Walker's fears. I was trying to present the Gospel to him, but he swerved his bicycle out of my immediate reach and just gave me a big smile.

God had one rule for Adam and Eve in the Garden. They were not to eat the fruit of the Tree of the Knowledge of Good and Evil. I also had one rule for my Garden of Eden. I was not to leave the boundaries of my own yard. Like Adam and Eve, I also broke my rule.

Later Thursday evening or early Friday morning, I remembered my two Norman Rockwell coffee mugs that I must have imagined having pictures by Burl and Ives on them. Early Friday morning, while Mrs. Walker and Beryl were probably still asleep, I left them on Mrs. Walker's porch swing as a gift for them. Later that afternoon, as Beryl cycled by, he asked if I was the one who'd given them the cups. I admitted that I had. He thanked me; he didn't know my stay-in-your-own-yard rule.

After I returned from Broadmoor Hospital, I saw Beryl when I was taking a stroll through the neighborhood. I told him I had been hospitalized. I apologized for anything I had done or said when I was psychotic. I didn't use that word. Probably just said *sick*. He said no apology was necessary.

Scene 8: 144,000 Cars of Gold

Friday, June 1–Monday, June 4

On April 16, 2007, I met Gail and June, two Jehovah's Witnesses who were to become friends with my roommate, Alan, and me. I remember the date, because they were the first to inform me about the Virginia Tech massacre that day. They kept coming back to visit every week or so, because June enjoyed talking with Alan so much. After a period of time, I agreed to study one of their foundational books with Gail by phone on Saturday mornings. Gail told me they believe there will be only 144,000 people (mostly patriarchs and Jehovah's Witnesses) in heaven, and most of those have already been chosen.

Early each Friday morning, a house in my neighborhood that's catty-cornered to mine always has ten or so cars parked in their driveway or on the road in front of their house. I always wondered what was going on. A Protestant Bible study or prayer group? A Tupperware sales meeting? Jehovah's Witnesses planning their week? Not likely at a home rather than a windowless Kingdom Hall, but I chose the latter interpretation during my severe psychotic manic episode.

My neighborhood is quiet, with very little traffic, practically none on the street that runs in front of my house. Both from my yard and inside my house, I kept watching the cars coming and going down a side street and from that catty-cornered house. I imagined each car to be on a mission to carry out the Jehovah's Witnesses' plans organized at that house on Fridays.

During this scene of my psychotic episode, my house was at first in the Garden of Eden, then in the current Heaven, then later, on earth during the Millennial Kingdom, and then in the new heavens and earth that will be created after the War of Armageddon and the Great White Throne Judgment of nonbelievers. I was surprised that my mansion in these future residences would all be the same as my current earthly home (before the Rapture) and in the same physical location.

During the early part of this scene, while I lived in Eden, the cars looked normal, but on Sunday and Monday, as I viewed them from my den window, they appeared to be 144,000 in number and solid gold, as the streets in Heaven are described (Revelation 21:21).

As the World Turns

Now, the world don't move
To the beat of just one drum,
What might be right for you,
May not be right for some.

—Al Burton / Alan Thicke / Gloria Loring /
Robert Walden *Diff'rent Strokes* theme song

Wednesday, May 30–Monday, June 4

Theme: Game Show Delusions

Backstory

Because of cybersecurity issues, I'd dropped my internet and cable services in October 2017 and didn't add them back until September 2018. Since my house appears to have the TV antenna reception of a Diebold bank vault, I could only view two TV stations during that year—Testament of Truth TV (TTTV) Christian TV and a station that aired The Simpsons.

Since I wasn't interested in The Simpsons, I became a TTTV junkie. I'd never seen it before. I took lots of notes, made some donations, bought some CDs, DVDs, and books, and received gifts in return for most of my donations. So it's understandable that some of my psychotic episode motifs would revolve around my TTTV experiences.

These psychotic scenarios didn't follow a consecutive sequence pattern, because I would switch back and forth between them in a manner not unlike flipping channels with a remote control. The content was usually illogical and mostly just plain inaccurate. But I will report the scenarios as they actually happened.

I've chosen to collect some of the similar events and organize them into scenes with names of TV shows, many of which first aired in the mid-1950s, near the time I was born. These would be familiar to an older audience. I remember game shows such as *Queen for a Day*, *It Could Be You*, *To Tell the Truth*, and *Truth or Consequences*, as well as soap opera dramas like *As the World Turns*, *The Guiding Light*, and *The Edge of Night*.

I pretended that my imagined shows were videotaped from my front yard. This was inspired by all the cameras and lights I'd seen during the 2018 filming of an episode of Oxygen TV's *Mark of a Killer* at a house near the entrance to my subdivision.

Most of my shows were performed in my living room. I collected props from my dining room, kitchen, master bedroom, and den. When the "tapings" were taking place, I was facing the front windows with the drapes open and the living room lights turned on. Most of the tapings happened after dark, with many in the middle of the night. After each taping I would turn off the lights, but before I closed the curtains, I would go to the front windows, mix frankincense with coconut oil, and put it on my face. This was supposed to be a vanishing wrinkle cream.

Game Show 1: It Could Be You

I've chosen "It Could Be You" to describe the grafting of Gentiles who've accepted Jesus (Yeshua) into the olive tree representing God's chosen family tree of believing Jews (Romans 11:11-24). Meemaw3 completely distorted this passage and represented the grafting as a drafting, similar to that of the NBA or NFL, except that the last one drafted selects the next pick.

The idea of grafting into Israel's "favored nation" family tree came from the "Grafted-In Symbol" (sometimes referred to as the "Root Symbol") on my 50" x 60" woven throw. I received two of these for the $500 donation I made for humanitarian aid to the Maghrebi Jews in North Africa. I gave one throw to Hilary, one of my two close Jewish friends.

Since this part of my psychotic episode distorts and blasphemes Christian theological truths, I want to set the record straight before I describe the scenes in this TV game show.

The Grafted-In or Root symbol was discovered in the area around Jerusalem. It was used as a decoration on pottery dated by archeologists to the second century AD. The symbol unites a menorah, a star of David, and a fish, and symbolizes the relationship in Jesus (Yeshua) between Jewish believers and non-Jewish believers (Gentiles). Those of us who are Christians are automatically grafted into the tree of the remnant of Judaism who accept Yeshua (Jesus) as the son of God (Yahweh or YHWH).

The menorah represents the Torah (Jewish written law; the first five books of the Christian Old Testament). The Star of David signifies that Yeshua (Jesus) will reign over the kingdom of David. And the fish symbol represents Christians and Christianity. The Root Symbol means that Christianity has its roots in Judaism, and we are all branches of the same tree:

> But some of these branches from Abraham's tree—some of the people of Israel—have been broken off. And you Gentiles, who were branches from a wild olive tree, have been grafted in. So now you also receive the blessing God has promised Abraham and his children, sharing in the rich

nourishment from the root of God's special olive tree (Rom. 11:17 [NLT]).

Game Show Rules

Robot Meemaw3 established two Jewish Roots trees, one originating from each of my two close Jewish friends, Hilary and Rachel. Hilary is a computer programmer, and Rachel is a well-published New York Times Book of the Month Club author. I draped my root symbol woven throw over a solid oak rocking chair on the right-hand side of my entertainment center and a tallit over a straight-back, cane-bottom chair on the left side. The rocking chair represented the ones grafted/drafted in through Hilary, and the straight-back chair portrayed the people drafted in through Rachel.

I remember most of the people I used for grafting, but I don't remember the order in which they were drafted. I will list them in an odd sort of "logical" order, which might have been how they were actually picked. In my mind, each person was selecting the next one to be drafted in through them. Some of the choices would be totally impossible in reality. According to my rules, any member of a draftee's real family could automatically be pulled in through their branch. Thankfully, Mom (Effie Jordan) grafted me in!

I alternated choices for each side, but I will describe the drafts for each side separately. I always used an object—picture, book, snow globe, paperweight, CD, or something—to represent each person that was selected. This object was placed on the chair during the time I introduced the draftee to the TV audience, making them the "star for a few minutes," as in the show *Queen for a Day*.

The Jewish family trees are listed below with the object used to represent each member while on the chair stage. The object was moved from the chair to a prop holding area (couch, dining room table, bed, or den) after each person's minute of fame. Some props were used more than once.

Hilary's Olive Tree Family

Person	Prop Representation
Hilary	Woven throw with root symbol
Hillary Clinton	*Hillary Rodham Clinton (Encyclopedia of First Ladies)* by Deborah Kent
Donald Trump	Washington, DC snow globe and a plexiglass Iwo Jima paperweight
Jonathan Cahn	*The Paradigm: The Ancient Blueprint That Holds the Mystery of Our Times* by Jonathan Cahn
Larry Huch	*One New Man* CD

Hilary was represented by the throw because I gave her one just like it. It's obvious why a Hilary would draft a Hillary. Not so obvious that Hillary would pick Donald Trump, but they become good friends later in this looney psychotic experience. I could see President Trump picking Jonathan Cahn because of the subtitle of his book, *The Paradigm: The Ancient Blueprint That Holds the Mystery of Our Times*, which combines religion with politics by comparing similarities of ancient Jewish history recorded in the Bible with modern political events. When I returned from Broadmoor Hospital, the prop remaining in the rocking chair was the *One New Man* CD. I received that gift from Larry Huch Ministries at the same time I got the woven throw that covered the rocking chair.

Rachel's Olive Tree Family

Person	Prop Representation
Rachel	One of her earlier books
Effie Jordan	Small silver frame with Mom's picture
Don Jordan	A book by Don Jordan, columnist, author, and anthology editor
Rev. Jesse Jordan	Michael Jordan commemorative Coke bottle
Dr. Ben Carson	*My Life* by Ben Carson, MD (with Cecil Murphy)
Candy Carson	*A Doctor in the House: My Life With Ben Carson* by Candy Carson
Mark Lowry	*A Very Candy Christmas* CD with "Mary, Did You Know?"

Rachel's book was opened to her picture on the inside cover. I'm sure she "picked" Mom because of the story I'd sent Rachel, "The Surprise Gift," which I wrote sometime around Mom's death in the late 90s. I put a 2" x 3" framed picture of Mom in Rachel's chair beside her book, where it remained until I returned from Broadmoor.

I picked Don for Mom because of his last name. He is my other famous author friend and teacher. I chose my pastor, Reverend Jesse L. Jordan for Don because he has been one of my spiritual mentors. In addition, Don, his mother, and a few of our mutual friends attended our church the Sunday I went forward during the altar call to become a member. I chose the Michael Jordan commemorative Coke bottle to represent him because one member of our church is such a devoted Michael Jordan fan. It is also significant that three Jordans were chosen in a row.

The Carsons were a natural choice, since I'd answered text messages for his political campaign. I chose Mark Lowry because he wrote the lyrics of my favorite Christmas song, "Mary Did You Know?" sung by Candy and Craig Aven on her Christmas CD. I thought Mark, like King David in the Old Testament, must be a man after God's own heart (1 Samuel 13:14). Later, after I heard him sing "Old People," a song he co-wrote, on a Guy Penrod TTTV program, I decided, "I've got to meet this guy!" I tried to go on his Spring Fling Cruise, but when I tried to register, it was already full.

Game Show 2: The Price Is Right

This show ran concurrently with my "It Could Be You." Since TV airtime is expensive, I made separate commercials for the two Olive Tree grafts. They were taped and shown randomly between draftings.

TTTV programs and associated ministries are funded in a variety of ways. Some will send you a CD or book for a gift of any amount. Most sell books, CDs, DVDs, and Bible study guides for various amounts, depending on how they are packaged. A book, workbook, and accompanying CDs might be $99, but you could get the entire package plus another series for $160, $38 below the catalog value, if you buy the day the show is aired.

Some of these items are written and recorded by the show host, and frequently they include resources from their guests. Sometimes they show pictures and videos of the adults and children being served in the foreign humanitarian ministries they support. Occasionally, the host will become emotional when he or she describes the poverty of people served by their ministry. Other times, the host or announcer will suggest that if you benefit from their teachings, you might consider becoming a monthly partner. I personally think this is the most effective way to solicit donations. The ministry can project monthly revenue in charity financial budgets and reports. St. Jude Children's Hospital published in 2015 that it depends on private donations for seventy-five percent of its operating expenses, with an average donation of about $35. I suspect this model holds for most of the ministries on TTTV.

In this "The Price Is Right" psychotic scene, the two Olive Tree grafts competed for funding from the commercials I made. When imaginary viewers "called in," they would designate which charity (Olive Tree family) they wanted to support. I put a Longaberger rocker doll cradle basket in front of the rocking chair (Hilary's tree) and the doll cradle my father made me when I was about four years old for the donors to Rachel's tree.

I'd moved the book *The Three Billy-Goats Gruff (A Norwegian Folktale)* from the right-side armoire of my master bedroom suite to my now unmade bed with many other props and books I collected from various parts of my house. This folktale reminded me of the second crude video game I'd made during a three-day weekend jam for the Ludum Dare competition in 2014. It was a platformer video game, in the style of the original Mario Brothers game, except that mine didn't work, and there was no way implemented to keep score. I never finished it, but I tried to sell it in this psychotic game show adventure, anyway. I'm sure it was one of my for-a-donation-of-any-amount products, since it was of no value to anyone.

Perhaps the most valuable item I tried to sell was a numbered (28852) box set, *The African Queen, Limited Commemorative Edition.* It contained eight collectible lobby cards with Katharine Hepburn and Humphrey Bogart, a restored and remastered copy of the film, a hardcover edition of *The Making of the African Queen* by Katherine Hepburn, and a copy of the shooting script by James Agee and John Huston. I have a collection of James Agee books, but I didn't try to sell any of them.

In one of my "The Price is Right" mock TV programs, I had two guests who are MDs—Elijah and Maria, my friend Betty's daughter. I'm not sure if they'd won a Nobel prize for their cancer research or if they had successfully separated conjoined twins, as Dr. Ben Carson pioneered, but they were represented by a statue of a doctor putting on surgical gloves and two booklets I'd found earlier in the Longaberger basket. One had to do with twins, and the other was a "People's Health Series" pamphlet, which I find ironic given my mental state at the time. It was entitled "Phosphatidylserine (PS): Mental Clarity at Any Age."

The only money collected that I'm aware of was $5 in the *Rachel basket*. Since I sometimes store money in a clean diaper while I'm traveling, I had taken an unused panty liner, removed the paper backing, and stuck a $5 bill to the back of it. Elijah found that as I stood looking on the day he and Nicole brought me home from Broadmoor. I tried to explain. He just shook his head.

Game Show 3: To Tell the Truth

During the writing of this section of my madness journal, I chose this game show to represent the psychotic experiences I imagined involving three political figures: President Donald Trump, Senator Hillary Clinton, and Benjamin Netanyahu, Prime Minister of Israel. I will sometimes refer to them as the *Trump Trio*. I don't intend to make any political statements here, though I find the rules of the game to be humorous in this context.

Panel Game Show Rules

This actual TV game show had four celebrity panelists and three contestants or challengers. The challengers were to try to stump the panel as to which of them had an unusual occupation or experience. The panelists asked them questions related to the sworn affidavit by the central contestant, who was telling the truth. The two impostors were allowed to lie. Prize money was split between the three contestants based on the number of wrong votes by members of the panel.

It's not surprising that these psychotic vignettes centered around the nation of Israel. Since I began watching TTTV in September 2017, I've learned many things about the Jewish religion and customs through such shows as "The Jewish Jesus" with Rabbi Kirt Schneider, "Jewish Voice Ministries International" with Rabbi Jonathan Bernis, "Larry Huch Ministries" with Pastors Larry and Tiz Huch, "Zola Levitt Presents," and from Rabbi Jonathan Cahn, who is often a guest on TTTV.

At 3:00 a.m. on December 20, 2017, I watched a show on TTTV with Todd White as a guest. I'd never heard of him before. They showed video footage of him witnessing to Jews and Muslims just outside the Temple Mount in Jerusalem. Days later, there was a skirmish nearby, and some of the Jewish guards were killed, including one that had talked with Todd. I think hearing this story is why my psychotic episode was so obsessed with the Temple Mount.

In my delusions, the Temple Mount was most often located at one of the two front doors to my house, but sometimes at the apex of my subdivision where an Oxygen TV episode had been taped, or at Covington Fellowship Church in Charlotte. Other times, I thought it was at the corner of my lot, at the east gate of Eden (Genesis 3:24), or at one of the twelve gates of the New Jerusalem described in Revelation 21 with the names of the twelve tribes of Israel written on the gates.

My Biblical concepts were all messed up, but I was consistent in describing who the players were in this "To Tell the Truth" scenario. Sometimes during the "It Could Be You" and "The Price is Right" games, I would abruptly stop to let the Trump Trio go to the Temple Mount to dedicate something. It could be the dedication of the new Israel Embassy in Jerusalem. It could be the dedication of the Third Temple, which hasn't been built yet. In any case, the Trump Trio was shattering glass ceilings.

I always carried three props when I went to one of my front doors with the Trump Trio. I carried a mezuzah with a Roots Symbol on it for PM Netanyahu, an Iwo Jima paperweight for President Trump, and Hillary's volume of the *Encyclopedia of First Ladies* with her picture on the cover.

The Game of Life

Saturday, June 2–Monday, June 4

Theme: Existential Video Games

Backstory

As with earlier sketches, the following two scenarios played out in a random fashion, in no particular order. I've decided to describe them as video games using the names of TV shows. These vignettes occurred almost exclusively in my den, though some parts occurred in my dining room, kitchen, and laundry room. I find it both odd, and a relief, that nothing happened in my office. Putting a ransacked filing cabinet in order would've been a nightmare!

In addition to books, snow globes, the ceramic hen I'd bought in Fancy Gap, and other props, my dining room table contained *showbread*. I didn't understand the significance of the show/shew bread at that time. I'd just recently heard the terms on TTTV. My bread was a stale biscuit in a plastic bag that was left over from the breakfast I'd eaten on Tuesday, May 29, at the Lakeview Restaurant in Fancy Gap.

Beside the bread was an almost-full seventeen-ounce bottle of Gold Emblem Lime Seltzer Water that was given to me by a stranger on the previous Thursday, May 24 at the Benton Convention Center in Winston-Salem, where I'd vomited uncontrollably all day. I believe my leftover Krystal chicken biscuit and tater tots breakfast on Wednesday, May 30, this leftover bottle of zero-calorie water, and the biscuit were all that I ate or drank until after I was taken to University General Hospital on Monday, June 4. I lost about 20 pounds that week. It was a blessing in disguise that I'd quit taking my medications. If I'd been taking the glimepiride and metformin to control my diabetes, my blood glucose level could have become dangerously low.

The most prominent piece of furniture in the den is an antique dresser with an odd-shaped swing mirror that belonged to my paternal grandparents. They were born in the late 1860s, so this heavy, handmade, solid walnut wood chest is probably about 150 years old. On either side of the swivel mirror are two small pedestal shelves, which I used for displaying pictures or a statue during this part of my psychotic episode.

The blue wingback chairs in the den had been moved to the sides of the room to accommodate two queen-sized blowup mattresses. I'd put one on top of the other to make the bed more comfortable for Tom, the homeless guy I'd taken care of for a few cold nights in December 2017. He had a softball-sized stage IV tumor in one of his lungs, making it hard for him to breathe.

I'd been out of town in much of early 2018, and my small, artificial, decorated Christmas tree was still situated on a tall cane-bottomed stool in front of the field stone wall that contained a large fireplace. On a similar stool were a pair of antique Oster hair clippers my dad had used when he was a barber (before he began farming), a small green-and-brown ceramic frog with warts on its back and legs, a random LEI power supply, a ZIP Firestarter (with the words: *lights instantly, lights even damp wood*), and a container of long-stemmed matches. I'd moved these items to the stool from the mantel over the fireplace. Seven medium-sized logs for building a fire lay on the hearth.

Two vintage Singer cabinet sewing machines played an important role in one of the crazed vignettes in this room. The drawers and stool compartment still had the original sewing paraphernalia my mom and mother-in-law had stuffed into their respective machines years ago.

Video Game 1: Days of Our Lives

In this domestic world, I thought my friend Betty was with me, but I didn't see her or hear her voice. I just felt her presence and probably talked out loud to her. I put something on the floor as a divider, maybe one of my canes or the knee-length metal shoe horn from the old milk can that my brother had decoupaged pewter green.

I played a game with Betty similar to the lotto game I played alone in the Toy Room. I sifted through the drawers of my mother-in-law's sewing machine and threw some of the stuff to see on which side of the boundary it landed. The items closest to me were keepers. I repeated the process with things in the compartment inside the stool seat for Mom's sewing machine.

The items included red, blue, yellow, pink, black, and white ric rac of various sizes, hem bias bindings, sewing machine needles and bobbins, several pieces of elastic in different lengths and widths, a wide strip of yellow Velcro, a screwdriver for a buttonhole maker, new buttons still on the card, and a red ribbon. Three plastic tape measures neatly held together with clothespins were in one plastic bag with my name written on it. Another plastic bag contained a vintage, two-inch-wide elastic belt with a beautiful gold and black metal butterfly closure that I'd never seen before.

My greatest find was a homemade item, which I called a "fancy pincushion pad" for lack of a better guess. The heart-shaped pad was 4" x 5" and consisted of a soft padding covered with shiny, dark-yellow satin cloth. The small cushion had an outer covering crocheted around it in a pattern with a large strawberry shape in the center of each side. Both my grandmother and my mother crocheted, so I don't know which one made it. It was edged with a quarter-inch shell stitch and had alternating pink and blue boundaries. Those colors made me think "*baby*," but I couldn't imagine what it would be used for. About 70 inches of one-inch-wide yellow matte-finish ribbon was looped through the crocheted covering near the top, tied in a bow, leaving a 32-inch loop. A similar bow with a five-inch loop was affixed on the back. I imagined they were for hanging on a wall, or wearing around the neck, though the longer loop would hang down to the knees. Now I know it was a sachet that contained a fragrance. It was put in a wardrobe or chifferobe to make the clothes smell better.

Betty was twenty years my senior. I vaguely remember asking her earlier in this domestic world what women used for sanitary napkins when she was younger. I don't remember what she said, but I think my mom had once told me that they'd made them from cotton rags or old sheets cut up in appropriate-sized strips and sewn together. Later in the day, I think I thought this sachet was a homemade feminine pad.

I'm confused about the puddle of blood my neighbors told the EMTs about when they picked me up on Monday. They examined my vagina at University General Hospital and found no evidence of injury. Who discovered the blood? Who cleaned it up? Could it have been pee? When and how did I use the sachet? I found it soiled when I returned home from Broadmoor Hospital and washed it with some other clothes before I thought to examine it.

Video Game 2: This Is Your Life

The idea for this game came from one of the books I bought for the Toy Room at a Goodwill store. *On This Day* is a beautiful cloth-bound children's gift book by Andree Dolan, with illustrations by Joanie Byrnehall. Birth information for a baby girl named Anna was filled in throughout the narrative of this book.

This is Your Life was an NBC radio show from 1948 to 1952 created and produced by Ralph Edwards. From 1952 to 1961, he hosted the reality TV show that evolved. Edwards would take his guests down memory lane with surprise visits by family, colleagues, and friends from their past.

My choosing some people to honor "On This Day" was a natural imitation of *This Is Your Life*. I began by moving the doilies, pictures, candelabras, and trinkets that usually cluttered the top of the antique dresser. I put some of them on one of the sewing machines and other knick-knacks on my dining room table.

The book *On This Day* stayed open on the first page, where Anna's name was written. I did not write in this book. Instead, I would sometimes record the honoree's name in the Book of Life in my kitchen.

I began by placing a mezuzah sent to me by Larry Huch Ministries (a Messianic Jewish ministry) on the top of a remote for an old, inoperative burglar alarm system that was affixed to the wall just inside the front door to the den. I thought this would protect my house from demons. I put a white porcelain statue of a man and woman embracing on the left pedestal shelf beside the mirror. I would place a picture, book, or other representation of the guest of honor beside the book on the dresser. After I spoke kind words about the person I was honoring, I would move the statue to the opposite side of the mirror and put a small picture of the person or something representing them on the left shelf. When another person was honored, the props would be cleared, and the statue would be moved to its original position on the left side of the mirror.

The next step is kind of vague. I did not always do the same thing. I would sometimes go to the kitchen and write in the Book of Life. Sometimes I would take the Eternal Flame candle to the living room window facing the road to do some sort of dedication. Other times, I would slam the front door beside the antique dresser. I have no idea what that signified. Once, a wooden frame with a cloth representation of the cross fell off the front of that outside door, and the frame broke. I also shattered the glass in a small framed school picture of Megan. I slammed the door hard enough to break a porcelain frame with a photo of Elijah's family when their first child, Sara, was a baby.

It rained throughout much of the day on Sunday and Monday. I would sometimes crack the door so my "This Is Your Life" guests and I could experience times of refreshing. This concept comes from the Scripture:

> Repent ye therefore, and be converted, that your sins may be blotted out, when the times of refreshing shall come from the presence of the Lord (Acts 3:19 [KJV]).

My first honoree was my son-in-law, Richard. I placed their wedding photo and daughter Calypso's birth announcement picture on the dresser beside the Dolan *On This Day* book. After the dedication, I wrote Richard's name at the top of the first page of the Book of Life and wrote these words in a Bible I'd been planning to give him: "Happy Zeroth Birthday in Christ! Jordan Family." Jordan was my maiden name.

Earlier in the week, I had played a match game in the den, whereby contestants were matched with a benefactor to win a free vacation. I imagined I would give them pictures or magnets that related to one of three philanthropists, Wesley, Dawson, and Rick. They were to go on a treasure hunt. Richard and Megan found Dawson, who volunteered to pay for a wedding trip to Italy, the vacation of their dreams.

Next, I honored my paternal grandmother, Sallie Jordan. I used the only photo I have of her. She is pictured with fourteen of her seventeen children. My grandfather and three of their children had passed away when this picture was taken. Two died from early childhood diseases and George's legs were crushed when he tried to hop a train when he was thirteen years old. Grandpa Henry died in 1919 during the Spanish flu pandemic, shortly before this picture was taken.

My dad was one of the youngest of their children. His sister Aunt Louise told me one time that when people asked her mother why she had so many children, she would say, "Because I don't want to go to heaven and have Jesus ask me why I missed an opportunity!" She would have freaked out if she had known she was born with a few million eggs and still had between 300,000 and 400,000 of them when she became of child-bearing age!

Probably because of his surname, I honored my pastor, Reverend Jesse L. Jordan by representing him with the same Michael Jordan commemorative "Share a Coke" bottle that I'd used before, when robot Meemaw3 grafted him into Israel's "favored nation" family tree.

I commemorated several other friends and family members, but the most surprising honoree was His Eminence Timothy Cardinal Dolan. He was to represent all Catholics. I used my copy of the book *Life Lessons from My Life with my Brother Timothy Cardinal Dolan* by Bob Dolan to represent him. Of course I chose him because of Andree Dolan, the author of *On This Day*.

Altered Reality

Your brain hallucinates your conscious reality.

—Anil Seth, *TED Talk*, ted.com, April 2017

Saturday, June 2–Monday, June 4

Theme: Psychosis in Virtual Reality

Background

As the week progressed, the psychotic scenes at my home grew stranger and more sacrilegious. Reluctantly, I decided to include these sketches to enable the reader to experience the entire episode as it happened.

When I'm manic, I often have flights of thought in normal conversations and generally find it difficult to focus. In a psychotic manic episode, these problems are exacerbated. My mind vacillates between scenarios, usually with little or no apparent rhyme or reason. I will experience one motif for a while, then go back to a previous one without any sense of connectivity. As a former computer programmer, I decided to model this chapter as if I were designing a virtual reality (VR) environment.

I was first introduced to VR programming at a Supercomputing Conference in the early 1990s. I sat in a chair, put on a headset, and I became a red corpuscle traveling throughout a human body. I specifically remember being inside the heart. The experience was vivid, but static. I didn't have control of my environment. This passive reality was much like the scenarios I experience during a psychotic manic episode.

My most recent VR encounters had been playing games using Elijah's HTC Vive system. It allows me to walk around with my headset and hand controllers and manipulate my virtual space. Sometimes I can move around between the rooms that make up my VR world. I feel like I'm *there*, sometimes in an expansive area, though I know I'm really within the physical confines of my 3D space. I might be walking out of a window of a tall skyscraper to pick up something at the end of a plank. It's frightening, though my mind knows it's not real. In the Google Earth VR game, my body could be flying above the earth to any location, maybe to hover over my own house or go to Japan. You feel as if your body is actually flying at a high rate of speed. Terrifying!

One difference between these static and dynamic VR experiences and a full-blown manic episode is that, though VR simulations might seem real to me at the time, my mind soon tells me that they are not true. In both of these VR types (static and dynamic), I experience the emotions and reactions I would have if the adventures were actually happening to me.

In contrast, I liken a motif similar to this in my psychotic world to a dream-like state while I'm awake. It's just like the dreams I have at night, in the sense that thoughts and experiences I've had before can sometimes be strung together randomly to form a new narrative. The difference between my dreams and psychotic adventures is that I don't recall most of my night visions and dreams. And I don't recall feelings and emotions from my psychotic sagas. I'm assuming I didn't experience any. I was able to write this diary because I did so soon after my psychotic episode, while I remembered so many of the details. However, in some of the later, and even intermediate, stages of a psychotic episode, I don't remember many of the details.

Virtual Reality Game 1: Another World

I began designing and playing the virtual reality video games in my den that I thought Elijah and my oldest granddaughter Sara (age six) were programming for his HTC Vive system. I lay on top of the double air mattresses, trying to visualize worlds as multidimensional hypercubes. I have no idea what diverted my attention to hypercubes. Maybe I saw my books *Flatland* by Edwin A. Abbott and *Sphereland* by Dionys Burger in one of the bookcases beside the air mattresses. These fantasies deal with the fourth dimension and higher. I'm sure I didn't try to read them. My mind was too far gone for that!

I tried unsuccessfully to remember exactly how a four-dimensional hypercube (tesseract) was constructed. I was getting very frustrated, but I continued to make the worlds without understanding what they might look like. I just considered that one of the edges was connected to the seam made by the stone wall and the adjacent paneled one. The worlds were connected to my den with a substance that was as thin as a spider web.

When the fourth-dimensional world was ready to launch, it would slowly begin moving toward the corner where the two walls meet. Finally, one vertex of the tesseract would become attached to the top corner of the room, connected only by a thin, small thread at one of its vertices. When I was ready, I would clip the filament and send it sailing through the atmosphere out to a four-dimensional universe.

Now I know to visualize a tesseract similarly as I see a 3D cube. The cube is to a square as the tesseract is to a cube. The cube has six square faces and eight corner vertices. The hypersurface of a four-dimensional hypercube is made up of eight three-dimensional cubical cells. I can see why I couldn't figure it out. My mind wasn't batting a thousand at that time.

I can't remember what I put inside the hypercubes. I remember thinking I was cutting the thin, spider web rope of one of the worlds to give to my neighbor Judy. I asked her to take it home and begin to populate it. I don't think she was actually in my house. I just felt her presence there.

Another time, I was making a world that reminded me of one of the first Vive video games I'd ever played. It was called *The Accountant*. I don't hear well when the volume is low, so I didn't know how vulgar the language was. Those in the room who could hear and see on a computer screen what I was seeing in my virtual space were telling me what to do. My punishment for losing in one of the levels was the guillotine. I had to get down on the floor and put my head into what looked through my virtual reality goggles to be a real guillotine. After the snap, I was taken into a virtual reality room with a burning forest fire. At first, I didn't see the trees for the fire, so I exclaimed, "Oh, no! I went to Hell!"

When I was almost finished with one of my hypercube worlds, I designed it to be burned up like in *The Accountant*. It was the last room in my virtual reality game, and I was ready to burn the world down and start over to make a new one.

There were seven pieces of firewood on the hearth in my den beside the air mattresses where I was designing the new games. I found the fire starter and long-stemmed matches on the nearby cane-bottomed stool, so I proceeded to try to strike a match. Fortunately, I have always been afraid of fire and matches, thus I was not successful after a few strikes. I decided to go to the kitchen to get the butane stick lighter I'd used to light the Eternal Flame candle.

All of a sudden, it dawned on me! Elijah is sort of a *pyromaniac*. He has always been fascinated by fire. As a kid, he collected lighters, and he now juggles and twirls fire as a form of entertainment for his friends. How could I deny him the pleasure of burning up my virtual reality video game world?

I imagined he actually came to my house. It was raining cats and dogs, but I didn't worry about the dampness not being conducive to fires. I cracked the door and handed him my car key fob and the butane lighter as he *headed* for my car. Somehow, my virtual game world had enlarged. I gave him the mandate to burn down the whole earth. After all, it was just a video game, and I was about to design a new world to take its place!

Virtual Reality Game 2: Creation Myths

Myth #1: Leviathan Lays an Egg

I'd found an alligator earlier in the week during the toy sort. This stuffed animal was made in China. Her covering was multicolored—differing shades of green, yellow, and brown. Her comical eyes looked like half-chartreuse, half-white balls with a black, hard plastic center. She looked like a sea monster, so I called her Leviathan. Leviathan was referenced in the Hebrew Bible (Christian Old Testament) in the books of Job, Psalms, Isaiah, and Amos.

How did I know my Leviathan was a female? She has a Velcro slit the length of her belly, which opens to expose a single white egg about the size of a ping-pong ball. It's attached to the inside of her stomach with another piece of Velcro.

The story I imagined for this myth is unclear. I remember thinking that the sea monster came up out of a chaotic, watery abyss and presumably deposited her egg somewhere. This would become a newly populated world.

Myth #2: Iggy Procreates

On one of the days in Andree Dolan's legend book, there was a drawing of a beautiful winding river that reminded me of playing as a kid in the icy cold waters of the Ball Creek that ran through one of our farms. Somehow, the salmon in that picture reminded me of a gift to me from Alex, one of Megan's friends when she was in high school.

Iggy™ is a Ty Beanie Baby® iguana. My Iggy was born on August 12, 1997. He's about a foot long and has blue-green fur, beady yellow eyes, and a wide, lime-green mouth. His olive-green dorsal spikes make a convenient handle for carrying him around, reminding me of the scruff of a cat's neck. His tag says he likes to sit on a rock and bask in the sun.

So I got the idea of letting him create a whole new world. Why not? I thought Iggy was swimming upstream in Ball Creek to fertilize nests of fish eggs that the females had created. I took off all of my clothes, and Iggy and I crawled between the two queen-sized air mattresses on the den floor. Iggy became aggressive. I didn't know iguanas can bite so hard you sometimes need stitches, or I would've let him swim alone.

When I came out from between the mattresses, I imagined I could feel the cold primordial water flowing over my body. I was lying on the floor, presumably in a shallow part of the creek. On my den floor around me, I could see the big rocks with slick, wet moss that my brother and I used to sit and play on in the Ball Creek. I could smell the clean air and hear the soft babbling and burbling sounds the water makes when it passes over the smaller stones.

At first, there were tadpoles swimming all around me. Soon they became frogs hopping from one stone to the other. I was confused about Iggy's species. He appeared to morph between lizard and fish and frog. I think I must have gotten the idea for birthing frogs from the ceramic horny toad on a cane-bottomed stool in my den.

I don't remember how long I lay on the floor with this hallucination, but at some point, I switched to another creation myth.

Myth #3: Calypso Is Born

As time progressed on Sunday and Monday, the details grew ever fuzzier. All week I'd been preoccupied with the special dedication of my granddaughter Calypso to take place at Covington Fellowship Church in Charlotte sometime around the End of Time. I was inviting all Christians I came in contact with to attend.

The definitions of End Times vary among many world religions. I believed that Jesus would return to earth soon, but He would first rapture all believers who were dead, and then those still living would be caught up to meet Him in the air:

> For the Lord himself will come down from heaven with a commanding shout, with the voice of the archangel, and with the trumpet call of God. First, the believers who have died will rise from their graves. Then, together with them, we who are still alive and remain on the earth will be caught up in the clouds to meet the Lord in the air. Then we will be with the Lord forever (1 Thess. 4:16-17 [NLT]).

Calypso was to be the best baby to represent mankind before this earth is burned up and a new one is created in the eschatology I adopted for this myth:

> But the day of the Lord will come as a thief in the night; in the which the heavens shall pass away with a great noise, and the elements shall melt with fervent heat, the earth also and the works that are therein shall be burned up (2 Pet. 3:10 [KJV]).

Her dad, Richard, named their daughter Calypso because he's fascinated with superheroes. In this myth, I mixed theology with mythology. I fancied that Richard was the Greek Titan god Atlas, who was condemned to hold up the heavens for eternity after being defeated during a war against Zeus.

I did not know these details at the time. I just thought he came up out of the deep, cosmic abyss to become the father of Calypso, whom he named for the Greek goddess-nymph in Homer's *Iliad and Odyssey*. She had entertained the Greek hero Odysseus for seven years. Atlas was not born of a woman. He, Megan, and Calypso would become a new first family released into a new world—a strange new Adam and Eve hybrid race.

129

It was finally time for Calypso to be born. Her mother Megan wasn't at my home, so I decided to sit in for her. Unfortunately, Calypso was breech, so I tried to turn her around using a handicap reach extender.

I think I must have been experiencing a temporary bipolar blackout when I tried to put the grabber part into my vagina. I was not aware of my surroundings or actions.

PART V

HELP I'VE FALLEN AND I CAN'T GET UP

Meemaw3

June 4–18, 2018

Healing on Hold

As he headed out for Naioth in Ramah, the Spirit of God was on him, too. All the way to Naioth he was caught up in a babbling trance! He ripped off his clothes and lay there rambling gibberish before Samuel for a day and a night, stretched out naked. People are still talking about it: Saul among the prophets! Who would have guessed?
—1 Sam. 19:23-24 *THE MESSAGE* (MSG)

Monday, June 4–Thursday, June 7

A Grim Discovery

Monday, June 4, 7:40 p.m.

Finally, on Monday evening, Rick, who has a key to my house, came across the street to check on me. That was when he found me naked on the floor, trying to insert the reacher-grabber tool into my vagina, and promptly called Megan and 911.

Before the ambulance arrived, I remember talking with his wife Judy and Leslie, their young female boarder. Leslie was crouched on the floor beside me. She told me not to be concerned. She was a mental health counselor and was there to help me. After asking my permission, Judy climbed across the scattered stuff strewn throughout my ransacked house and found a white, floor-length fleece robe in my closet. She asked me to stand up and put it on, reassuring me that the men on the emergency medical services (EMS) team were coming into my house with their backs to me.

I remember being wheeled out of my house on a gurney and put in an ambulance. I recall the stick of the IV and the blaring, wailing sounds of the siren. From the back window, I saw trees rushing by as we sped toward University General Hospital less than ten minutes away. We arrived at 8:10 p.m.

Hospital Admission

This is how most stories end in the hospital. Not with crash carts and sirens and electric shocks to the chest, but with an empty room, a crisp white bed, silence.

—Jacob M. Appel, *Phoning Home*

133

Monday, June 4, 8:30 p.m.

There was a long blackout period, during which I can't remember anything that happened after I was taken out of the ambulance. I don't remember punching a police officer in the face, knocking his glasses to the ground, and then trying to kiss him on the mouth. I don't remember that or anything else that happened at University General Hospital until sometime after I was pre-screened for an involuntary admission.

During that screening, I was put in a green gown so I would be easily recognized if I tried to run away. My memories of my entire stay at University General Hospital are sketchy at best, and the medical records I was given didn't fill in the gaps. The most detailed records were from the Preadmission Screening and T-Sheet Documentation.

Preadmission Screening

Monday, June 4
8:30 p.m. Triage
    Vital Signs taken
    Pertinent Information: pt found by neighbors in floor naked, ems states "pt house was torn apart and pt was laying [*sic*] in floor placing some form of object in vagina and pt was talking in some form of manic state" pt during triage talking in intangible sentences and seems to be in a manic state not answering questions
    Put in a green gown and moved to a safe environment
    Patient unable to sign "Patients at Risk for Suicide/Elopement" Form.

8:45 p.m. ECG

9:10 p.m. Chest X-rays

9:20 p.m. Blood drawn for Labs
Gave Haldol 5 mg IV, pt mildly calmer, but will not be able to perform a pelvic exam at this time. Will give Geodon 10 mg IV now.

Note: *This is the only record of antipsychotic drugs being given during my entire stay at University General Hospital. Geodon was given 1 hr 10 minutes after I arrived at the hospital ER. The exact time Haldol was given was not documented.*

10:30 p.m. Urinalysis and Alcohol/Drug Screening

10:45 p.m. CT scan of head
Tuesday, June 5
4:45 am   Plan for psychiatric admission

T-Sheet Documentation

Chief Complaint

CHANGED MENTAL STATUS The patient has been disoriented and confused. (Per EMS, pt was not seen by neighbors for 2 days. Neighbors went to house today and found pt naked on the floor w/some vaginal bleeding. Pt had a trash grabber next to her and was noted to be trying to put grabber in her vagina. History is limited as pt is altered and disoriented to person, place, and time. Per medication list, pt is on Lamictal for bipolar disorder, and apparently has not been taking any medications.

Spoke with son who states pt has had manic episodes in the past (most recently in the 1990s) which include removing all items from her house and speaking frequently about God. Neighbors noticed pt took everything out of her house and called pt's daughter regarding her wellbeing. This started today, unknown when patient was last known well and is still present. (unknown) The patient was not found unresponsive. No alcohol recently or recent drug use. No weakness or numbness.

Progress and Procedures

04:41 06/05/18. Labs WNL, CT Head, CXR, EKG WNL. Pt likely w/acute manic episode at this time. Plan for psychiatric admission.

Clinical Impression

Severe manic episode with psychosis

Physical Exam

Appearance: Odor of alcohol is not present. Speech is not slurred. The patient is not agitated.

GU: Chaperone present (female CNA present). Normal external exam. Speculum exam normal. Genital inspection normal. No vaginal discharge. No vaginal bleeding.

Blackout Ends

We don't yet see things clearly. We're squinting in a fog, peering through a mist. But it won't be long before the weather clears and the sun shines bright! We'll see it all then, see it all as clearly as God sees us, knowing him directly just as he knows us!

—1 Cor. 13:12 (MSG)

Monday, June 4–Tuesday, June 5

The first thing I remember is being in a room all by myself, lying on a gurney, possibly strapped to it, no doubt still in a green gown. In 1983 and 1995, I think I'd been put in a straitjacket to prevent myself from hurting myself or others. At those times, I was also secured to a gurney in some fashion.

This time, I was probably not aware of my confines. A restrictive environment wouldn't have bothered me because of the delirium going through my mind at the time. I felt I was being given a complete blood transfusion from Jesus' veins. I probably thought I was lying still on this gurney because of the imagined complex vein surgery. I believed they were connecting me to Jesus, one vein at a time, and using some of his infinite supply of blood to fill mine. This isolation room was beside a hydraulic door. I began hearing this door close, and that loud, clicking sound became that of an imaginary, huge staple gun sewing each of my veins back together after filling with Jesus' blood.

This theme began during a dream I had on Saturday night, May 26 at the B&B where I stayed in Kernersville, near Winston-Salem. It was after the last night of the Power and Love event, where I'd had a significant encounter with God. Still reeling emotionally and spiritually, I felt I was getting a new supply of blood from Jesus. It was to be a literal blood covenant, not unlike the covenant renewed during the observance of Holy Communion.

The dream was triggered by the hymn "There Is a Fountain Filled with Blood" written around 1771 by William Cowper, who coincidentally suffered greatly from mental illness. This hymn was written during a time of depression and was both one of his most beloved and simultaneously controversial hymns. This hymn was based on a verse in the Old Testament book of Zechariah.

Washing Away Sins

On the Big Day, a fountain will be opened for the family of David and all the leaders of Jerusalem for washing away their sins, for scrubbing their stained and soiled lives clean. (Zech. 13:1 [MSG]).

The idea of a blood transfusion was not at all what the Scripture or hymn are about. The first stanza of this hymn shows its influence on this psychotic scenario from the deep recesses of my mind.

> There is a fountain filled with blood
> Drawn from Immanuel's veins;
> And sinners plunged beneath that flood,
> Lose all their guilty stains.

After the *transfusion*, I remember being wheeled on a gurney through a long hallway. Several people accompanied me. Talking incessantly and thinking about the *Game of Life* virtual reality video game that I had designed near the end of my time at home, I told them Hitler was in heaven. I believed I was designing the virtual reality video games that Elijah and Sara were programming. Sara was addicted to creating Minecraft worlds, so to me that qualified her—at age almost-seven—to be a programmer for the *Game of Life*. At the end of each game, I could begin again and design another world. In the next world, Hitler could have been programmed to spend eternity in hell with Satan and his demons.

Elijah later told me I caused quite a stir with that one! The University General Hospital staff didn't understand that it was just a video game.

I was being transported to an isolation room, which had only a tall exam table with a gray vinyl covering and no paper or cloth sheets. No other furniture. No TV mounted on the wall. No windows. Just a door that remained locked. The table was about the size of a regular flat casket and just as stark and cold.

During this retention period, I experienced a time travel motif. I thought a family member had to go back in time and procreate in each generation to jumpstart a *beget sequence* for our family that repeated in each successive generation.

This was reminiscent of a hallucination I'd experienced at the first psychiatric hospital where I was a patient at the end of 1982. My mind was racing very fast then. It felt as if it were running backwards in time. I thought I was the antichrist, and I had to go back in time all the way to creation and commit every sin that had ever been committed. That was a trip! This explained why the nurses were always having to make me stop taking my blouse off in the hallways. My skirt, which I'd purchased earlier that day for about $500 with a tailored suit at a fancy clothing store in North Palm Beach, didn't fit and was zipped up only part way. My psychiatrist later told me I couldn't have been the antichrist, because that was his ex-wife!

The Holding Pen

Amid Shortage of Psychiatric Beds, Mentally Ill Face Long Waits for Treatment.

—Michael Ollove, Pew Research Center, August 2, 2016

Tuesday, June 5–Thursday, June 7

Tuesday, 6/5/2018 10:13 a.m.
S: Pt. is currently sleeping. Zach, RN, reports no issues at this time with the patient. Pt. does have many home medications listed in medication history.
O: VSS. Pt. sleeping. No distress.
A/P: Will start home medications listed in history. Pt. awaiting psychiatric placement.

Sometime before 10:00 a.m. on Tuesday (probably around 5:00 a.m.), I finally reached the *maximum security* suite of about ten rooms. There I would spend the next couple of days awaiting transfer to a hospital that accepted older patients with mental health concerns.

There were only two such hospitals available for me in this area. The closest one, Broadmoor Regional Hospital, about an hour and a half away from my home, had a Geriatric Psychiatric Unit. It treats patients with dementia and mental illness together in the same geriatric ward, which is common. I wasn't accepted for transfer to this hospital until Thursday. It was another full day there before I started taking the antipsychotic drug olanzapine (Zyprexa) on Friday evening, which ultimately led to my healing.

It was over four days after my neighbors found me until I was actually treated with this antipsychotic drug for my severe psychotic manic episode.

My first recollection from my holding pen cell is being locked in a room with no windows—only a low, immovable bed with sheets and a small, flat-screen TV mounted high in one corner of the room. I was fed regular meals, which I ate sitting close to the floor on my low bed. Because of my hand tremors, sometimes I dropped my food and made a mess. I would take off the soiled bedding, and the person who came for my tray would supply me with clean bed linen. I had to hide the leftover condiments I was saving for no apparent reason, except that I'm a hoarder.

There was an observation/workstation room for the RNs and other staff members in one corner of the suite of holding cells. It remained locked at all times, and sometimes it was difficult to get their attention by knocking on the door when you needed something. There were no call buttons. I was reluctant to knock on the door because I was afraid that if I caused trouble, they would keep me longer.

The observation room was probably 12 feet x 12 feet and was encased in tempered safety glass from about four feet up. Beside the room was a locked hallway, maybe 12 feet x 6 feet, which led to a large, automatic, garage-type door opening upward to the outside of the hospital.

Elijah came to visit me on Tuesday afternoon. He lives in another state about four and a half hours away. He'd been on a business trip and gone out of his way to visit me. One of the staff members (probably an RN) went outside the building to meet him. He told Elijah about the "Hitler in heaven" fiasco and the "punched a police officer" incident. I had no attending physician in the Holding Pen for Elijah to talk to, just nurses and the PA who signed the three short notes that were included in my medical records.

We were allowed to visit for about five minutes, ten tops, in that locked hallway. We sat across from each other in metal-frame stack chairs. The staff observed us through the observation glass. I'm not sure, but the visit and conversation might have been videotaped. There was no apple pie with a file! The staff member came in and asked Elijah to leave promptly when his time to visit was up. Elijah came in and left through that locked garage door.

I don't remember much of our conversation, just the parts about Hitler and the policeman. I told him about the virtual reality video games that he, Sara, and I were making. Each time I said something wacky, he would give me his characteristic smile, wink, and nod. I interpreted it to mean he agreed with me. It was the staff that didn't get it. They knew nothing about video games.

Elijah also told me I would be transferred to Broadmoor Hospital the next day, and I would really like the place. I don't know why I wasn't moved there until Thursday—possibly waiting for a bed, insurance company pre-admission approval, or the availability of a police car to transport me. Elijah made an unproductive trip to Broadmoor on Wednesday. Due to his work schedule, I was unable to see him for another week and a half, right before I was discharged from Broadmoor.

Wednesday, 6/6/2018 1:53 p.m.
S: Pt. is wanting to take a shower. No other requests. Pt. does have inappropriate behavior, but has not been aggressive.
O: VSS. No distress.
A/P: Awaiting psychiatric placement.

Tuesday evening and much of Wednesday are a blur. I speculate that I slept much of the time. At some point, my TV was turned on and I was given a remote control, but no instruction on how to use it. It was complicated. So I watched only one channel with no sound or closed captioning.

I continued my psychotic video game scenario of taping commercials for TTTV. It bothered me a little that the characters were always the same. I believed that we just dubbed over the dialog to fit the advertised product. Later, a staff member told me how to change channels, but I preferred the one I was originally watching.

Sometime on Wednesday, my room was unlocked, and I was permitted to leave my room to go to the bathroom unaccompanied and walk around in the hallway. But I couldn't go in any room but my own. The doors to many of the rooms were cracked open a bit, and I noticed that many patients appeared to be sleeping. I suspect we all slept a good portion of the time we were there.

I only saw three other patients walking around freely, like I did. We became friends. Doris was fifty-something and had a good sense of humor. Once, she came to her door and gave me something from her tray that she didn't like, maybe a banana or a tangerine. I had lost about fifteen pounds during my episode, as recorded in the ER on Monday. I lost another three to five pounds in the Holding Pen, despite the fact that I always ate everything on my tray.

My other two new friends were young men, probably in their twenties. Robert didn't say much. He had a big, endearing smile and repeatedly laughed in a high-pitched, silly-sounding voice. He would go to the door of the observation room and get their attention for me. I was afraid to bother them myself.

James didn't say much either, except that he wanted out of there! None of my friends appeared to be psychotic. Their diagnoses were not evident to me. Their speech was not pressured. Maybe they had been suicidal. Maybe overdosed.

The staff had promised Doris and me that we would be transferred on Wednesday evening, but the two males were released instead. We were sorely disappointed. I told her about breaking out of a long-term care facility in 2012, but added that it would be impossible to get out of our Holding Pen. She acted like she was going to try. When I woke up late on Thursday at 9:30 a.m., she was gone. I wondered how she did it!

I find it incredible that there were only three entries in my medical records pertaining to the three days they kept me in the Holding Pen awaiting psychiatric placement. All I remember them doing was feeding me, taking me to the bathroom at first, and giving me my home meds. No vital signs taken. I wasn't permitted to take a shower. I don't remember if I wanted to take a shower for hygienic reasons or if it was part of my video game psychosis. I'd taken showers at home to reflect changes in game motifs.

Thursday, 6/7/2018 9:23 a.m.
S: Pt. is currently sleeping. No issues reported by Gina, RN.
O: VSS. No distress.
A/P: Pt. has been accepted to Broadmoor. She has been awaiting transport to the facility.

My time in the Holding Pen ended at 11:00 a.m. on Thursday. Two policemen took me to Broadmoor Hospital. I was in the back seat with bulletproof glass or plastic separating their prisoner from the front seats. I didn't realize it was a police car until Elijah told me later when he visited me at the hospital. Guess I thought it was an Uber or something!

141

Pathway to Sanity

High high in the hills, high in a pine tree bed.
She's tracing the wind with that old hand, counting the clouds
with that old chant,
Three geese in a flock
one flew east
one flew west
one flew over the cuckoo's nest.

—Ken Kesey, *One Flew Over the Cuckoo's Nest*

Thursday, June 7–Monday, June 18

Landing in the Aviary

Thursday, June 7
Psychiatric Condition: Bipolar disorder with severe mania (HCC) with history of psychosis.

The seventy-five-mile trip was quiet and without incident. It was a beautiful sunny day, and I enjoyed looking out the window at the green pastures and trees and the pretty colorful flowers. You wouldn't know I was experiencing moderate mania by my conduct. I was quiet and didn't even try to talk to the policemen through the hole in the bulletproof barrier that separated the front and back seats. We arrived around 12:30 p.m. I was pleasant and thanked them for the ride. They accompanied me inside and transferred my custody to the Geriatric Psychiatric Unit.

Compared to the Holding Pen at University General Hospital, this place was a Ritz-Carlton! Noting that I was wearing only a long, white fleece robe with no panties, Ashley, an RN, went to a storage room and returned with a pair of red pajama bottoms—ironically covered with pictures of Eeyore, the old gray donkey in *Winnie-the-Pooh*. She also found a suitable black knit sleeveless top and a red cardigan sweater to wear if I got cold. Most important to me, I got my first pair of hospital-issue panties. I don't know why University General Hospital didn't give me underwear.

A pleasant surprise awaited me inside. Elijah had come the day before, because he'd been inaccurately told I would be there. The Broadmoor staff asked him for pictures of my family to print out for the wall facing my bed. One was of my son's entire family at an amusement park, and the other was Megan and all four of my grandchildren playing with a bubble machine in her kitchen.

I was always alert and polite when the staff came into my room to take vital signs, give me meds, or ask medical history questions. They were indeed surprised when I lost it right before dinner! I was standing facing the large window that reached from about four feet up the wall to the ceiling. I hadn't stayed in a room with a window to the outside world since I'd left my house on Monday, June 4. As I stood close to my window, gazing out over the parking lot, I had a sense that there was someone else in the room. I turned around abruptly, and an elderly man, whom I'll call Howie, was only about three feet behind me, staring at me with that eerie look. I screamed at the top of my lungs! Then I started chasing him out of my room, yelling repeatedly—"Get out! Get out!"—until I had shooed him out of my room like a fly.

Poor Howie! I scared him half to death. The RN and CNA didn't know which of us to calm down first. They explained Howie's behavior to me. He paced up and down the hallway, sometimes wandering into other patients' rooms. Once, he pooped in my bathroom and didn't flush. At least I thought it was him. It could have been one of a few other geriatric patients with dementia.

Journaling Begins

Psychiatric Condition (2:45 a.m.): anxious mood; affect is not angry, not blunt, not labile and not inappropriate; tangential speech, hyperactive; not agitated, not aggressive, not slowed, not withdrawn; not actively hallucinating and not combative; paranoid; not delusional; impaired cognition and memory; impulsive; not depressed; no homicidal or suicidal ideas; attentive, abnormal recent memory.

Thursday, June 7–Friday, June 8
On Friday, I spent most of the day and evening in my room, except for three meals in the day room. I kept myself busy making copious notes. I became obsessed with learning everyone's name. People like it when you can remember their name.

I'd begun on Thursday evening by asking each person who entered my room the name they preferred to be called. I wrote it down with a short description of them on one of the Broadmoor letterhead notepads that I found in a drawer. One example was: Cynthia (Cyn), RN with salt and pepper hair. As the week progressed, I would add a description of the scrubs they were wearing to help me try to distinguish the RNs, CNAs, NPs, and PAs. For example, Shauna, CNA, pigtails, navy blue swirly and figured top with solid light blue bottom. Later, I realized the scrub wardrobes changed from day to day. I made more notes and charts about the staff than any other subject of my notes while I was there (about twenty percent).

My notepads were filled with more than one topic per page, about fifty little pages, some front and back, including writing on cardboard backings. I asked some of the staff that I trusted most for some blank sheets of letter-size paper. In total, they gave me about 30 additional sheets of paper. I drew horizontal and vertical lines on some of them to make grids resembling spreadsheets. I kept having to change them as I learned more about each staff member. I would have asked one of them to help me, but I was always hiding my work in a drawer. I was paranoid that they would find out and fuss at me or, worse yet, take away my pen and paper. I made four folders from the larger sheets labeled Staff and Patients; Timeline; Hymns; and Misc. I even had a calendar spreadsheet, which I made to help me keep up with the date and the day of the week.

On Friday, my psychiatrist added a new medication, olanzapine 5 mg, which I took at bedtime (8:40 p.m.). This was the first antipsychotic medication I'd been given since my neighbors found me on Monday evening.

Waste Can Latrine and the Grand Ole Opry

Psychiatric Condition: manic without sleeping well, hyperverbal but pleasant on approach. talks constantly, jumping from one topic to the other, doesn't appear paranoid; flight of ideas; depersonalization perception; impaired recent memory; distractible; impaired insight and judgment.

Saturday, June 9
My CNA for the Friday night shift was gruff and had a poor bedside manner. I thought of her as Nurse Ratched from *One Flew Over the Cuckoo's Nest*. Due to my paranoia, I was afraid of her and felt that I couldn't trust anyone on that shift. Sometime in the night, I inadvertently locked my bathroom door, probably thinking it was the door to my room.

I usually wake up frequently during the night to pee. When I woke up at 4:30 a.m., I realized the door to my bathroom was locked. No problem! I could use the potty chair in one corner of my room. When I got there, I discovered it was a potty seat with no pot. The last thing I wanted to do was use my call button to ask Nurse Ratched for assistance!

Being a problem solver, I decided to use the large paper cup on my nightstand. I sat in the potty chair and urinated in the cup. I carried it to the opposite corner of the room and poured it into the waste can that was across from the door to my bathroom.

The non-slip socks they had given me were way too big. Probably would fit a man's foot size 12. I stepped on the protruding end of one sock and tripped and fell against the wall, hurting my head. The staff heard the noise and came running! They discovered the pee in the waste can. Nurse

Ratched fussed at me for sitting on the waste can to pee and falling off. I insisted I hadn't done that and described how it had happened, but some of the staff didn't believe my explanation. I had a large hematoma on the back of my head, but the CT scans and X-rays were normal. Later, Nurse Ratched became one of my best friends. I think we both learned you catch more flies with honey than you do with vinegar.

As the day progressed, my psychosis subsided. Though I continued to make lists and experienced symptoms of severe mania, the content of my notes became less delusional. The antipsychotic medication was working after only one dose!

At lunch, I met Evelyn (Eve). She was eighty-seven or eighty-eight, I've forgotten. She didn't hear well, but we were able to communicate if I sat on the side of her good (better) ear. We hit it off right from the beginning. I made it a point to sit with her at dinner, too. I learned that her husband, two brothers, and she had formed an ole time gospel music singing group in the fifties. They performed at the Grand Ole Opry on the same stage as The Chuck Wagon Gang (CWG), one of my all-time favorite groups. She told me that people have told her that her range was even higher than the CWG's soprano, Rose. Rose could get pretty darn high!

All I had to do was mention to Ashley that Evelyn used to sing on the Grand Ole Opry, and she sprang into action, organizing an old-fashioned gospel music singalong after dinner. Eve motioned for me to come sit by her, and we led the group singing, she with her high soprano voice and me with my limited, five-note range alto. We sang songs like "I'll Fly Away," "The Church in the Wildwood," "Farther Along," and "Will the Circle Be Unbroken." We sang *a cappella* and with no written music. Eve must have had perfect pitch. She would say, "Let's sing it with 3 flats" (E-flat major) and she'd give me what she called 3 pickup notes. We almost couldn't get her to stop singing so we could go to bed! She kept thinking of others she wanted to sing.

Ashley finally told her we could sing again the next night, and we did. Finding music in songbooks became my obsessive preoccupation for the next day.

Sunday, June 10
Psychiatric Condition: *less manic; doesn't appear paranoid; and socializes well out of her room.*

I found a few hymn books in the bookcase in the dayroom and spent some of the day feverishly writing notes for the singing we were to have that evening. Counting fronts and backs, I made about twenty-five pages of notes.

I selected songs I thought Eve would know and enjoy singing. I picked all-time favorites like "Swing Low, Sweet Chariot" (a popular African

American spiritual); "Beulah Land" (a reference to Heaven); "Jesus Saves;" and "Jesus Is All the World to Me." I noted the book, the page number, the key, the number of sharps or flats, and the letter names of three or four pickup notes. I made three copies by hand of the final choices, one for Ashley, one for Eve, and one for me.

We had lots of fun singing. Eve's son picked her up to take her home before breakfast on Monday morning. We didn't even get to say goodbye.

Monday, June 11
Psychiatric Condition: Full affect, good eye contact, alert and oriented x4 (person, place, time, and situation), speech nonpressured and somewhat tangential; slept well last night with the 5 mg of Zyprexa; appetite is good; denies SI and no AV hallucinations; did not require any prns; appears better.

Evelyn was gone, but I make friends easily. I'd already met three patients on Friday at meals in the dayroom during my severe manic times. Today I spent more time than yesterday in the dayroom and met some more folks.

Glenn (also known as Cecil) was schizophrenic. They kept him tied to a reclining mobile wheelchair, which they equipped with an alarm. He was always trying to get up. I talked with him as much as he was able to communicate. I tended to talk more with the staff than the patients, though.

On Saturday, I asked RN Donna if I could have a Bible. She gave me one she said I could keep. Today I found some Bible commentaries in the day room. Most of the 66 books of the Old and New Testament had their own separate booklet, but some of the Minor Prophets and Letters of Paul had to share.

I read parts of a few of the commentaries and made some notes about the book of Mark, which also made references to Acts, Daniel, and Isaiah. On the top of one of my letter-size pages, I wrote "God's Grace in Mark." Jesus introduces himself. Peter says "He is the Christ (also Messiah or Yeshua)" (Mark 8:29). A Roman centurion exclaimed, "This man truly was the Son of God!" (Mark 15:39 [NLT]).

On a few random pages of notes, I wrote the chapter reference, Jeremiah 31. I looked it up. This is an interesting chapter to read in its entirety about God bringing the Jewish people back home to Israel.

Tuesday, June 12
Psychiatric Condition: Full affect, good eye contact, smiled when greeted; alert and oriented x4; speech nonpressured and still tangential at times; slept poorly last night; appetite is good; denies SI as well as any AV hallucinations; will double dose of Zyprexa to 10 mg; Still appears to be in a hypomanic state.

Much of the day I stayed in the dayroom talking with patients, but more often with staff. One of the nurses, Debra, had a dry sense of humor. She and I were always making puns and obscure references. She was so much fun to be with. Debra and Ashley, the class clown, were my favorites.

The Piano Teacher

Wednesday, June 13

Psychiatric Condition: full affect, smiled when greeted, alert and oriented x4, speech nonpressured and goal directed; slept much better with the increased dose of Zyprexa (10 mg); good appetite; denies SI and no AV hallucinations; does appear better.

Ashley wanted to learn to play the piano. Someone had pasted the letter names for a couple of octaves on the piano in the dayroom. She particularly wanted to learn how to play "Just a Closer Walk with Thee." I used to teach piano when I was in high school, but you'd never know it by the way I play now. The staff kept wanting me to play something; once I played something by ear (without music) to convince them I couldn't play anymore. No one challenged me on that! But I did still know music fundamentals.

Ashley couldn't sit down at the piano and let me teach her anything while she was working, so I wrote out extensive notes of what I would say if I were teaching her. For example, "The key of C has no sharps or flats. It is the easiest of the scales to play. CDEFGABC." I drew pictures of the treble and bass clefs and wrote the letter names on a staff. I went into too much detail; she probably could not understand by reading it on her own. But I gave my notes to her.

She'd given me a copy of the sheet music for "Just a Closer Walk with Thee." It was in the key of B-flat (two flats). I transposed it to the key of F (one flat), which would have been easier for her to play and sing. I only transposed the soprano (highest) notes. I wrote down all the words and put the letter names above them, but later decided it would be easier to read if I put them below. So I made a new page. I did this all in my room without a piano. I gave it to the staff to give to her; she wasn't working on the day I left the hospital.

Gimme That Ole Time Religion

Thursday, June 14

Psychiatric Condition: full affect, good eye contact, alert and oriented x4, speech nonpressured and goal directed; denies SI and no AV hallucinations; no delusions evident and appears to be coming out of the manic episode since starting the Zyprexa which is now at 10 mg.

I don't remember how it started, but we had a "revival meeting" in the dayroom on Thursday evening. We were singing, giving our testimonies, and praying with patients and visitors to get saved, so they could live in heaven with God throughout eternity and have a close personal relationship with Jesus Christ while living on earth.

RN Cynthia found some gospel music on YouTube, and we sang along. Lindsey went to another floor to get Patsy, the supervisor of the geriatric unit staff, who is a born-again Christian. They had brought her to my room on Saturday night to meet me. She knew of a Pentecostal event somewhere in Knoxville that was being broadcast, and she and I watched some of it on her iPhone, singing along with the praise and worship music.

I asked Imogene, one of the patients, if she wanted to receive Jesus as her personal Savior. That terminology was foreign to her, but she said, "Sure."

We got halfway through a repeat-after-me prayer for salvation, and she exclaimed, "Wait a minute! I've already prayed that prayer before." We discussed her salvation, and she started going around the room, giving her testimony, and praying for others to be saved.

There were probably a dozen people in the room, counting staff and visitors. I'm not aware of any professions of faith that night.

Imogene tried to talk with Glenn (Cecil) who is schizophrenic, but came to Patsy and asked her to present the Gospel to him. Patsy asked me to do it because she said I'd make a better presentation. I tried to talk with him, but he didn't have the mental capacity to pray a sinner's prayer. I believe that he won't be held accountable for rejecting God's free gift of salvation, paid for by Jesus' sacrificial death on a cross over 2,000 years ago. I think he will go to heaven anyway, like babies and people who are severely mentally impaired. I don't think it would have been against hospital policy for Patsy to pray for him, since I remember seeing some kind of wall plaque outside the nurses' station indicating a Christian denomination affiliation.

James was the only patient I prayed for healing for, but there were a few supernatural healings among the staff throughout the week. Brenda in Housekeeping was healed of arthritis. Lindsey, a CNA, was healed from back pain and asked me to pray for her father. He'd had seven discs removed. The

RN Christy was healed of glaucoma, and back and leg pain. I think Cynthia was healed of something at the Thursday night revival, maybe hearing and foot pain.

Sandra and Howie Blossom

Friday, June 15

Psychiatric Condition: full affect, good eye contact, alert and oriented x4, speech nonpressured; good appetite; denies SI as well as any AV hallucinations; really appears better; speech still somewhat tangential but this does not appear to be a problem.

In the afternoon, several patients were in the dayroom. Ashley got the idea to put some chairs in a semicircle and play catch with the ball. She kept lots of games and paraphernalia in one of the locked storage rooms. She brought out a beach ball about a foot in diameter. She sat in one of the chairs and tossed the ball to Howie. He knew what to do and passed it to another patient. He was smiling from ear to ear. No one had ever seen him smile. He had more fun than any of us. It felt so good to see him smiling like that.

After I returned home, I sent a letter to the Chief Nursing Officer, praising several staff members, but highlighting Ashley for playing games like pass-the-ball with us, and for setting up a miniature basketball hoop and bowling alley for us in the hallway. I copied the CEO and Chief Clinical Officer. The Chief Nursing Officer sent me a letter thanking me for the positive feedback and saying they would be honored at a district meeting.

Saturday, June 16

Psychiatric Condition: full affect, good eye contact, alert and oriented x4; good appetite; a bit tangential today; denies any thoughts of harming self or others; denies hallucinations; impaired insight and judgment; speech normal rate and volume; euthymic mood; distractible and impaired concentration; fair recent and remote memory.

Howie paced the hall many times each day. I asked him if I could walk with him, and he nodded yes. I had never heard him talk, and presumably the staff hadn't either. I walked with him many times after this before I left on Monday morning. I began counting our steps, and much to my surprise, he counted with me. When we got to the nurses' station, I pointed out to them that he was counting. They were surprised, too.

Sandra had been a patient there as long or longer than I had. She had never been out of her room. After I had such success with Howie, one of the nurses asked if I thought I could get Sandra to come out of her room. I said sure. I like challenges.

I began by sticking my head in her room and saying hello. Then I worked up to "May I come in?" We had a long chat. To her it was as if I were visiting her in her own home. She kept apologizing that she didn't have anything to give me to eat or drink. Then she remembered she had an unopened Ensure, which she insisted I drink. I was reluctant, but I didn't want to hurt her feelings. After all, she wouldn't starve if I drank it, and it was chocolate!

She told me to come back anytime. I could tell she really enjoyed our visit. I asked if she wanted to walk with me down the hall, but she wasn't ready for that step. She said she didn't think she could. I told her that we would walk the next time I visited her.

Elijah and Nicole Visit

The staff at University General Hospital had told Elijah that I would be transferred to Broadmoor on June 6. He was out of town for business, but he drove a long distance out of his way to be there when I arrived. Unfortunately, my discharge from University General was delayed for one day. I barely missed him! His work schedule prohibited him from visiting me at Broadmoor until ten days later, on June 16. Nicole and he brought me the one piece of unopened luggage in my bedroom, which had clothing of minimal use. I guess seeing my house, with random items erratically strewn throughout, was shocking enough to deter them from actually packing a new bag. They probably knew I would be discharged in two days, so I'd only need one outfit and a pair of shoes. It would have been nice to have some underwear too.

I had no other visitors while I was at Broadmoor. I was so happy to get to visit with them and even happier on Monday, when they came back to take me home.

Sunday, June 17

Psychiatric Condition: appropriate eye contact; converses easily; a little hyper conversational; denies any thoughts of harming self or others; denies any hallucinations or delusions; reports that she will feel as if some dreams are real at times, but states that she is aware of reality; she is at her reported baseline per family.

Sunday afternoon, I moved two chairs from the dayroom to the end of the hallway. Sandra's room was near the other end. I went to her room and told her about the chairs. And to all the staff's and my amazement, she walked with me all the way down the hallway. We sat there and talked a while before we came back. I told her my son and daughter-in-law would be coming the next day to take me home, and I wanted them to meet her.

I kept my promise. She had the biggest smile when Elijah talked to her. It made her day!

Free at Last, Free at Last!

Monday, June 18

Physician Discharge Summary:
Ms Manning was referred to Broadmoor Hospital by University General Hospital after she was brought to them by EMS in a manic episode. During initial interview she was still with pressured speech and flight of ideas. She admits to stopping her medication as she felt no longer the need for these. Lamictal was continued at 200 mg po bid and due to poor sleep and continued mania Zyprexa was started at 5 mg po qhs and after 2 nights went to 10 mg po qhs. With this change she showed a rapid recovery. Her sleep was much improved, speech was nonpressured and goal directed without the tangential character. She was alert and oriented x4, stated she felt well, had a good appetite, denied SI as well as any AV hallucinations and there was no sense of delusional thinking. Throughout her stay she did not require any prn medication but for the occasional Tylenol. I feel she has reached maximal benefit and will discharge today back to her home. Son will transport.

But leaving Broadmoor was bittersweet. I had made friends with many of the staff there, and I knew I would miss them. I had formed a psychological connection with my "captors" that could almost be compared to someone with Stockholm syndrome. In a weird sort of way, I felt like I belonged there.

The thing I remember most about that day was the ride home. Nicole had been reviewing my bank records, and soon after we left Broadmoor, she called me out on some of my restaurant expenditures. So much for empathy and the healing process! She knew very little about mental illness, and she didn't understand my feeble attempts to explain the extravagant tips. How could she?

I felt embarrassed and remorseful. These emotions were magnified later when we arrived at my home, and I had to try to explain the disarray throughout my house. Elijah and Nicole tried to straighten the house up a little so I could get back to some semblance of normal. I remember feeling uneasy. I knew I wanted to write about my psychotic episode and I wanted everything left as it was until I could make some more notes. But I didn't protest. They were just trying to help me. After they left, I was on my own. Back to my independent, hermit-like lifestyle.

Fortunately, Broadmoor had made appointments with Mr. Ed for the next day and Dr. M two days later. I continued to see them biweekly throughout the rest of the year. Mr. Ed and I discussed my feelings of rejection, guilt, and self-criticism. Dr. M monitored my tolerance for the antipsychotic drug, olanzapine. He gradually decreased the dosage from 10 mg, down to 5 mg, and ultimately to 2.5 mg daily.

I attribute my progressive, step-by-step, nonlinear return to near baseline by Thanksgiving (November 22, 2018), in part, to these two men, and resuming the coping strategies I developed in 2013 for a lifestyle that minimizes my bipolar symptoms.

PART VI

LIFE AFTER PSYCHOSIS

Meemaw1 and Meemaw2

June 19, 2018–Present

Just Push Refresh

Like recovery itself, acceptance is a process—something that happens in increments over time.

—Ken Duckworth, MD, *you are not alone, The NAMI Guide to Navigating Mental Health*

Refresh time varies from person to person and from psychotic episode to episode. It depends on the severity of the psychosis, the length of the hospital stay, and whether the underlying causes and conditions go away. I bounced back from my psychotic break in 2018 to somewhere between baseline and hypomania in record time!

On June 19, my first morning back, I drove myself to an appointment with my longtime psychologist, Mr. Ed. I continued to drive myself everywhere I went. I drove over 500 miles round trip to visit Megan and Elijah from August 4 to August 14.

With Mr. Ed's encouragement, I resumed much of the lifestyle management plan I had followed before this 2018 psychotic episode, including regular eating and sleep patterns, always taking my medications as prescribed, and asking my family and friends to help monitor my bipolar symptoms and behavior.

After my psychiatric hospitalizations in the 1980s, I would soon return to my job as a supercomputer analyst, but my performance didn't meet my expectations. After one episode, I lamented to one of my bosses that I felt guilty because I wasn't as productive as normal. He said my seventy percent was better than the one hundred percent for everybody else.

But this time, I returned from Broadmoor Hospital at near one hundred percent—or so I thought. But I was still moderately manic. Euphoric. Energetic. Increased activity. Armed with copious notes from my psychotic episode, I set out to write the definitive work about bipolar psychosis. I'd read other people's accounts of what an extreme bipolar psychosis was like, but they were not chronological and only described random, brief encounters. Mine was to be all-inclusive.

In the month and a half after I returned home from Broadmoor, I wrote about 140 double-spaced pages—from which Parts III and IV, and some of Part II, were extracted—and sixty pages about my hospital stays chronicled in Part V.

At the same time as this post-Broadmoor writing spree, I was busy with activities other than writing almost every day—doctor's appointments, lunch or dinner with close friends, nursing home visits, seminars, water aerobics, and balance center classes. I don't know when I found the time to do all of that manic writing. I was obviously still at the lower end of moderate manic. But by the end of July, I had cycled down to hypomania.

This writing marathon was only surpassed in 1979, when in twenty-four hours (with no sleep), I wrote the last fifty or so pages of my 200-plus-page mathematics dissertation, typed them (using text and symbol balls of an IBM Selectric typewriter), made copies, and delivered them to my PhD committee members, a fifty-mile drive away. I don't even believe this one myself! But it's true, I think, unless I was psychotic. But that was over three years before my first psychotic episode at the end of 1982. This behavior was clearly an indicator of prediagnosed mania.

Curious about the results of the potential personal healings others prayed for me at the Winston-Salem P&L event, I made an appointment with my ENT doctor on June 19 for a comparison test of my hearing and on July 5 with my orthopedic surgeon for an x-ray of my hip to see if the titanium pins had miraculously disintegrated. The results for both were negative.

My other activities were not so dramatic, except I continued to pray for healing almost everywhere I went. At Dr. M's office, on the University General Hospital campus, I prayed for a blind woman and a severely deformed young man in a wheelchair to be healed, but I saw no dramatic healings there.

Winnie didn't contact me again until late June 2018, shortly after I'd returned home from Broadmoor. He texted me to say he had never had anyone talk to him like that and that God would never forgive me for what I had said. He said I'd called him the devil, but it was me who was the devil.

I just replied that I'd had a nervous breakdown (terminology he would understand) and that Mr. Ed had suggested we not have a social relationship right now.

His texts had caught me by surprise. He's not the forgiving type. But just the fact that he'd reached out at all showed he'd missed having a friendly relationship with me. We had been close friends for 28 years. I don't know if it was because of my recent psychosis, or unresolved anger, probably a combination of both, but I didn't feel the emotions I would normally have felt about the healing of such a meaningful and important relationship. It was broken, and I was numb, unfeeling, and unforgiving. From childhood, I had always strived to make everyone like me, but this relationship had become too toxic and dangerous for me. All I felt was fear and indifference.

We talked by phone a couple of times after that. He was always the one who initiated the call. The last time, Winnie said I was a good person, and we should let Brandon take us to dinner sometime. I told him I thought I was too vulnerable. I might have another breakdown. My response was honest. I had thought I was healed of bipolar disorder in 2016, and this psychotic break in 2018 had shattered my faith and fueled my fears of having another severe bipolar episode.

I sometimes wondered how I would react when Winnie died, if I outlived him. I told myself he always waited until the last minute to make important decisions, and that he would probably have a deathbed conversion.

I can always remember the date Winnie died: 1-21-21. A palindrome! I was numb when Mia called to tell me. She had just received the call from the rehab facility. I think I was the first person she called. She was sobbing so hard she could barely get her words out. I didn't understand a word she was saying at first, but she told me who she was, and instinctively I knew what had happened.

I stammered and admitted that I didn't know what to say to console her. So I bumbled and asked the hard questions:

What had killed him? She didn't know, but probably had a stroke.

Did he ever become a Christian? She began to cry harder. "I don't know."

Elijah surmised what had happened and hugged me tightly after I hung up. So did his oldest daughter, Sara, who was standing nearby.

To date I've not cried or mourned Winnie's death. I did donate $100 to a GoFundMe to help pay for his cremation. Evidently, he had cashed in his burial insurance, probably to support his pornography addiction.

I'm trying hard to forgive Winnie, though I will never be able to forget. Though we never discussed this, I believe his rejection of Jesus was tied to his addiction. He knew he would eventually have to break it if he became a Christ follower.

I believe Jesus understands that addictions are complex diseases that are hard to heal, just like He understands some of the sins I've committed because of my bipolar disorder. Many people mistakenly think addicts just lack the willpower and could stop their addiction just by choosing not to do it. But that's just like people thinking those of us with bipolar disorder could overcome depression just by *thinking happy thoughts*.

When I approach Winnie's rejection of me, and more importantly of Christ, through this lens, I can say, as Corrie Ten Boom wrote in her memoir, *The Hiding Place*: "Forgiveness is an act of the will, and the will can function regardless of the temperature of the heart."

Jesus expressed it further as the ultimate step: "If you forgive those who sin against you, your heavenly Father will forgive you. But if you refuse to forgive others, your Father will not forgive your sins." (Matt. 6:14-15 [NLT]).

I console myself by thinking there might be a Winnie the Pooh 2 in heaven, even if he didn't tell anyone about his salvation before he left this earth.

On July 23, 2018, a month after I came home from Broadmoor, Tom, the homeless man who'd stayed with me for a few days in 2017, passed away. During the time he'd stayed with me, I'd met his cousin Jane by phone.

When Tom was dying, she asked me to meet her each day at the University General Hospital ICU. I wrote a eulogy for him, and Jane listed my name as a "special friend" in his obituary. Soon thereafter, Jane, her friend Vada, and I began meeting each month to minister to homeless people who lived in the same area where Tom had lived.

In early August 2018, I spent ten days in Charlotte. I attended two worship services and one seminar at Covington Fellowship Church. During the next three months, while in Knoxville, it was mostly business as usual—doctors' appointments, visiting or lunch or dinner with friends, business meetings with professionals, church services and gatherings, ministering to the homeless with Jane and Veda and at a nursing home with Charles, and I attended two weddings. I often prayed for healing. At one of the weddings, a woman with cancer said she was healed just before I began to pray for her, and a man with a torn Achilles smiled and thanked me profusely for praying for him. I didn't ask if he was healed. I visited family in Charlotte two more weeks around the time of Megan's birthday and wedding anniversary.

Nicole never did find out about Tom, but she DID find out about the temporarily houseless man Charles, a drug dealer turned lay preacher. Charles, his wife, and their three children stayed with me for a couple of weeks in February 2019 while they looked for permanent housing. I'd met him at one of the Men's Prayer Group meetings I attended.

Nicole fussed at me, saying, "How do you expect me to take care of you if you do these kinds of things? Why didn't you tell me?"

I told her that forgiveness is easier to get than permission.

Elijah told her, "You might as well accept it. She's been bringing in people who need a home all of my life, and she's not going to change now."

I don't think Nicole ever found out that I marched with Charles and a small group of fellow Christians for a mile around the most dangerous part of the housing project where he'd grown up, praying for the vilest of gang members who lived there. When I passed by a convenience store, I recognized the name as the one where a man had been murdered the week before during a drug-related robbery. God was definitely looking out after me! At a later point during the march, I started crying. My walking partner asked why. I told him I'd just realized that in 2012 I lived in a long-term care facility and used a walker much of the time. I'd just walked at least a mile without any walking aid.

Later, I would meet Charles each week at a local nursing home, where he preached, and we prayed for residents individually.

In early July 2019, almost one year after my psychotic break in 2018, two of my realtor friends were visiting me. I mentioned that someday I wanted to move to be near my children and grandchildren. They suggested that if I wanted to sell my house, the summer would be a good time to do it.

There were only three weeks left in July, but I impulsively told them I could be completely packed and moved by August 1. I actually finished packing and supervised $10K in repairs by mid-August. I did all the packing myself. My friend Melanie, Betty's daughter, and her three grown sons helped me get rid of almost all of my furniture, many books, and lots of other items I didn't need. She had a huge garage sale!

During the time I was selling my house in Knoxville, I contacted Megan's friend, who's a realtor in Charlotte, in hopes of buying a place to live near my children by the time I moved. Naïve dream! I moved in August 2019, though I didn't have a place to live. I stored my belongings at Megan's. I divided my time between my two children's homes, mostly keeping my luggage in my car.

I began receiving emails from Zillow, but nothing in my price range was satisfactory. Tired of living out of my car and being a burden on my family, at the end of 2019, I decided to rent an apartment on the Covington Fellowship Church campus while I looked for a house.

Then COVID happened! I quit looking for a place to buy. I was suffering from Covid paranoia (COVID-P) anyway, and I didn't want to leave my apartment to look at houses.

On December 11, 2020, the realtor called and said he'd found a suitable condo that was going on the market the next day. There were already fourteen people scheduled to look at it, but the seller's realtor agreed to let me look at it before it went on the market. Houses for sale were scarce at that time, and it would most certainly sell on the first day. I met the realtor at the condo, wearing my surgical mask/N95 double masking, and had a quick tour. I submitted an offer that night. The seller accepted it.

Because of my COVID-P, I didn't see the condo again until about a month later, right before we closed on January 11, 2021. I didn't even see the renovations the realtor supervised until right before I moved in on February 1. I finally moved my belongings from Megan's, a year and a half after I'd left most of them there. I had to downsize again in a drastic way, as my condo was about half the size of my former house.

Unforeseen Quarantine

*No one is alone in self isolation because the entire world is
there with you.*

—Ken Poirot

On March 1, 2020, I morphed into a Howard Hughes-Adrian Monk hybrid.

I first heard about the 20**19 CO**RONA **VI**RUS **D**ISEASE (COVID-19) soon after January 9, when the World Health Organization (WHO) reported a new mysterious pneumonia in Wuhan, China. But that was way over there and didn't really concern me. I might have whispered a half-hearted prayer for those affected.

I began to take notice when the first documented case in the US was confirmed near Seattle, WA on January 21. But I didn't know about the risk of a pandemic. That virus will never spread to the East Coast! It became REAL to me when I spent a few nights visiting Elijah and Nicole the last week of February. On Sunday morning, March 1, they recommended I go back to my apartment and self-quarantine. Elijah had contracted diarrhea and a fever after his night shift in the ER. He'd treated what he thought might have been his first COVID-19 patient, who had those symptoms.

I was concerned about Elijah and his family, but I told them, "I'm not afraid to die…because, if I do, I'll immediately be with Jesus. What could be bad about that?"

Almost simultaneously, they said, "Don't talk like that! Because if something happened to you, Sara would have a meltdown!"

Preoccupation with protecting Sara became an obsession. It made me super sensitive to totally isolating myself from the virus. A parallel mantra I kept reciting over and over was, "I can't become psychotic!" My family had enough to worry about without getting a call that I'd been found, naked as a jaybird, near the manmade lake behind my apartment—where another psychotic resident had been found a few years earlier.

My symptoms associated with COVID-19 correlated with my COVID-P (paranoia) reactions. Meemaw1 made the following chart to summarize my reactions to each perceived problem.

My friends and neighbors would have said it was impossible for me to be exposed to COVID-19. I was the resident who wouldn't even open my apartment door to the resident manager, the staff nurse, or other staff and residents during most of the year, even to talk through the gap in the door. Someone (usually the nurse) would bring my mail, put it in the plastic bag hanging on my doorknob, and pick up my trash, which I'd leave beside the door.

I would always use a Lysol wipe to touch the bag of mail and take it to my balcony, where I would leave it for seventy-two hours before even opening the bag. When I did open the bag, I would wipe each piece of mail with a disinfectant. I'd use a different Lysol sheet to clean all the doorknobs and surfaces I might have touched on my way to the balcony. Then I'd immediately remove my double masks by touching only the ear straps, being careful not to touch the front of the masks. I'd change my clothes and put them in my washing machine. I would usually take a shower. If I'd forgotten to sanitize something, I had to change clothes and masks and probably shower again. My skin got so wrinkly, I looked like a washboard!

COVID-19 Symptoms	My COVID-P Responses
Fever For adults (as measured by an oral thermometer): - Low-grade fever: between 98.6°F–100.4°F - Moderate-grade fever: between 100.4°F–102.2°F - High-grade fever: greater than 102.2°F	- If fever was suspected, I recorded my temperature every five minutes (or fewer) using both oral and ear thermometers - Alerted family if above 98.6°F - Texted prayer partners if above 99°F
Diarrhea	- Called or texted Nicole - Texted my brothers and some of my friends
Chills - Uncontrollable arm and leg movements - Felt excessively cold even after adding warmer clothing, more blankets, and adjusting the thermostat - Sweating - Shivering	- Thought I might have hypoglycemia, so I ate everything in sight - Called 55+ community nurse who lived down the hall at 3:00 a.m.; didn't know she was in a hospital; she called a neighbor to come see about me - Called Elijah at 3:00 a.m.; he was on shift at the hospital where he worked; he said to test my blood glucose level; it was normal
Nausea and Vomiting	- Sometimes I attributed to gastrointestinal or food allergy problems

Severe Fatigue **Muscle and Body Aches**	• Extreme weakness and tiredness • Needed assistance from Elijah and Nicole to turn over in bed
Weakness in Legs Unable to walk unassisted	• Needed much help from Nicole and Elijah to get from bed to bathroom • Later tested negative for COVID-19

In the early days of March, when I got my own mail and took out my trash, anytime I was outside my apartment, I always wore a pair of surgical gloves with a pair of rubber gardening gloves on top of them. I had three pairs of gardening gloves—neon green, turquoise, and fuchsia—which made me stand out, even from a distance. I put the disposable surgical gloves in a separate plastic grocery bag on the balcony to be thrown away after seventy-two hours. The rubber gloves were put in a black garbage bag, washed three days later with hot, soapy water, and subsequently disinfected.

I used Lysol sheets to clean the elevator buttons, handrails, door handles, or anything else I touched on the way to the front desk to pick up my mail. I carried three plastic bags: one for the mail; one with unused Lysol wipes (which I kept in a resealable zip-top bag), a large bottle of hand sanitizer, and two or three paper towels to blot the hand sanitizer, if needed; and a third bag to hold all the disposables. If I had packages, I would take my grocery cart and hang these three bags on the handles. Each time I would tell the clerk at the desk (even though I'd told them a bunch of times before) that I was only being that cautious because my son was an emergency medicine physician who was seeing COVID patients every day. And he was very protective of me because he was putting people on ventilators that were my age with even fewer comorbidities.

I was always embarrassed by my Howard Hughes-Adrian Monk persona. I justified it to myself by the admonition that "I couldn't let Sara down." I had to go to extreme measures to ensure I didn't get THE virus. Deep down, I knew that though this was the initial impetus, it had mushroomed way beyond that. I had developed a full-blown case of the dreaded COVID-P! I don't know who I thought I was fooling by shifting the blame to Elijah to try to keep me in the closet.

I even feared COVID more than breast cancer! On February 7, 2020, a mammogram showed a dense mass in my right breast. When Mom was my age, she'd had a radical mastectomy, which removed her entire breast and most of the lymph nodes under her arm. Nonetheless, Nicole, Elijah, and I reasoned that cancer would probably have a better prognosis for me than COVID. Elijah suggested I cancel a follow-up mammogram and sonogram appointment on March 20. I rescheduled for May 12, but the Imaging Center canceled that one because they'd shut down for the entire month of May due to the pandemic.

Later, I even debated about whether I should get a follow-up mammogram/sonogram on June 9, but I did. The mass had shrunk, and they even had trouble finding it!

I stayed paranoid during most of 2020 and into 2021 until two weeks after I received the second injection of the Pfizer COVID-19 vaccine. That was freeing. I felt like a little bird who'd just been let out of its cage. March 11, 2021 was D-Day for me...D-eliverance from COVID-P. It was amazing the difference just one day could make. After D-Day, I would often have to be reminded to put on a mask at places that required them. Sometimes I was inside before I noticed that other patrons were wearing them. It was a night-and-day difference from my former N-95/surgical mask duo days.

But then the Delta variant came on the scene in August 2021, and my COVID-P resurfaced. I got a booster shot on August 30. My ex-husband Steve was not vaccinated and died of complications from COVID on October 25, 2021. Though we divorced in 1990, I still loved him. He was the father of our children. Elijah honored his dad's wish to die at his home. He called me soon after his death. I went outside and sat on my deck for a couple of hours, crying and listening to music through my bluetooth hearing aids.

I became even more paranoid when the first case of the Omicron variant was reported in the US on December 1, 2021. It was highly contagious, and I was not protected by my vaccinations and booster.

Elijah contracted the virus in late December 2021. Due to overcrowding conditions in the ER where he worked, he was treating COVID patients in a janitor's closet, which had no running water. But there's no way to know definitively how he got it.

Around that time, a neighbor talked with me for quite a while when I went to my mailbox. It upset me later because we were not wearing masks. After that incident, sometimes I would wear an N-95 if I saw anyone outside when I took a walk or got my mail!

It was most surprising that I did not exhibit any symptoms of extreme mania or severe depression during the COVID pandemic. My paranoia and compulsive behavior around disinfecting and cleaning were the worst symptoms I had during this phase of the pandemic. Compared to my extreme manic bipolar psychotic episode in 2018, these symptoms were not bad at all. I would also get frustrated when friends and acquaintances would ridicule me for getting vaccinated or wearing a mask. I would try to avoid being in spaces where masks were neither required nor worn. This was the main reason I stayed inside my apartment in 2020. I should point out that many people who are not diagnosed with mental illness were experiencing paranoia and compulsive cleaning behavior during this phase of the pandemic, too.

Unbelievable Survival

COVID-19, are you going to be naughty or nice to me?

—Steven Magee

After years of antipsychotic, antidepressant, and mood stabilizer medication cocktails, combined with psychotherapy, Mr. Ed and I came to the conclusion that my faith in God, healthy interpersonal relationships, and positive life experiences probably played a more important role in controlling my bipolar disorder than the medications—though taking the prescription drugs exactly as prescribed was absolutely essential.

In September 2013, I'd developed a personal bipolar management plan to combine with my medications to improve my chances for success in dealing with this disease. In subsequent years, I've modified the plan some, as needed, but for the most part, I've tried to stick with the original program.

I believe that following this plan as closely as possible during my total self-isolation in the 2020 COVID-19 quarantine period, combined with taking my medications regularly as prescribed, kept me from becoming psychotic or needing any type of psychiatric intervention.

BIPOLAR MANAGEMENT PLAN September 2013 *I can gradually develop coping strategies and a lifestyle that minimize my bipolar symptoms.*

Lifestyle
Maintain a regular daily schedule and routine with balance and structure
(exercise, sleep, eating, work, Bible study, prayer, etc.).
Be organized in all life situations.
Stay focused.

Bipolar Monitoring
Self-monitor (watch for potential problems and relapses).
Ask friends to help monitor bipolar symptoms and behavior.
Always take mental health medications as prescribed.

Self-Perception and Acceptance
Build self-esteem; avoid negative self-talk.
Be determined, persistent, and patient with myself.
Learn to accept rejection.

Family, Friends, and Acquaintances
Strive for peaceful and stable family relationships.
Associate with positive, loving, and supportive people.
Don't isolate myself.

Recommendations
Don't talk incessantly, text excessively, or send long emails.
Pursue realistic goals; know my limits; don't take on too much.
Look forward; don't dwell on the past.

Coping Strategies
Minimize stress; talk to professionals or trusted friends and family members.
Engage in activities, hobbies, and volunteering.
Relax, laugh, and do fun things regularly.

Soon after I returned home from Broadmoor, I resumed following this bipolar management plan. Regular sleep times and amount are extremely important for managing bipolar disorder. During the pandemic, my schedule wasn't perfect. I would go to bed between 10:00 p.m. and midnight and get up between 7:00 a.m. and 9:00 a.m. I would usually fall asleep within minutes of going to bed, but a few times, like when I was worried that I'd contracted COVID-19, I had trouble sleeping until I took one or two Benadryls.

The other parts of my days varied widely. During the month of March 2020, I spent a lot of time FaceTiming with my three older grandchildren (ages four, six, and eight), usually for two hours at a time, but sometimes four hours, and once for six hours. We played hide-and-go-seek, with the one who was IT taking an iPad with them, as I suggested places to look. The girls and I played with Barbies. They all played video games using the Nintendo Switch, made Minecraft simulations, or used the FaceTime effects feature to make up stories and plays or picture designs for me, using lots of hearts with messages: "I love you, Meemaw" and "Hi, Meemaw!"

As time went on, home schooling put a damper on the long daily video calls, though for a while, shorter, two-hour calls continued two or three times per week in the evenings and on weekends. Gradually, by the end of the year, the video calls tapered off. Sometimes Calypso, my youngest grandchild, who turned three in April 2020, would ask Megan or Richard to call me for a Facebook Messenger video chat. I credit these video calls with my grandchildren as keeping me from feeling isolated and playing a huge part in keeping my mind straight.

Even though I was totally isolated in my apartment for several months, FaceTime, Messenger, Facebook, text messages, emails, and sometimes phone calls also kept me virtually connected to my brothers and many other close family members and friends each day. I also reconnected with friends and family members I hadn't seen or talked to in a long time. Our relationships grew ever closer. COVID-19 was a shared enemy! We exchanged the latest scientific data (original and contradictory revisions and redactions), jokes, memes, and political commentaries. Many *"I love you"* messages were sent. You never knew if that would be your last opportunity to say so.

I would alert Nicole, my brothers, and other friends and family anytime I was worried about my mental health. I forewarned them about what to look for and who to contact if they perceived problems. There was cause to worry a few times. Once, Nicole told me to chill for the whole weekend. No TV news. No internet searches about coronavirus or the number of cases or deaths in the counties where Megan and Elijah worked.

As an emergency medicine physician, Elijah was exposed to COVID almost on a daily basis. Megan was a pharmacist at an inpatient rehabilitation hospital that treated patients severely affected by the virus to help them recover. She sometimes had direct contact with the COVID patients.

I violated some of the rules in my bipolar management plan, but at the time, I believed many of the offenses were unavoidable due to the pandemic. How could I focus when the world was crashing down all around me? Who wouldn't be anxious about their children and their families when both were on the healthcare front lines? What about the suspicious mammogram on February 7, for which I didn't receive follow-up testing until June 9?

I didn't minimize stress when I took my temperature every five minutes or made pictures of the rash on my legs to send to Elijah to find out if it was a COVID symptom. I had trouble remaining calm when I found out I could have blood clots in my legs and would have to leave my apartment to make my first mid-pandemic public appearance at a dermatologist's office in a part of town where it's unsafe for me to drive. And what about the time I had a fever and wild spasms of arms and legs with chills a few days after being exposed to a Walmart subcontractor delivery driver on April 24 who didn't practice any of the COVID safety guidelines?

I didn't do all the activities and hobbies I would have liked to; however, at the beginning of April, I made a website which could have been used to rally the residents at my 55+ community around a common project of praying for our individual prayer requests and for people and issues related to COVID-19 in America—prayers for our leaders, first responders, necessary workers, researchers,…and to stop the spread of COVID-19. But since I wouldn't leave my apartment, I was not able to organize the project. I posted a link to the website on Facebook and emailed the link to a few of my friends, but received very little response. I also made two new blogs, ruthforthebroken.org and MeemawSurrendered.org (later changed to bipolar-life.org).

Amazingly, I think one of the things I did exceptionally well during this pandemic was to laugh. My family and friends have good senses of humor, and we kept each other amused with original humor, as well as exchanging funny emails, links, and memes. Laughter is even urged in the Bible: "A cheerful heart is good medicine, but a broken spirit saps a person's strength" (Prov. 17:22 [NLT]).

Why did I become psychotic in 2018 and not in 2020? I think it boils down to: "Was I taking my psychotropic medications?" and "How well did I follow my bipolar management plan?" It's instructive to compare the similarities and major differences.

In 2018, I believe the major difference was my inability to handle the rejections by Winnie. In addition, I didn't have a regular daily routine of exercise, sleep, eating, Bible study, and prayer. I was neither organized nor focused. I didn't pursue realistic goals. I talked incessantly and sent long emails and texts. I made long road trips. I attended two religious conferences in separate states within three months.

In 2018, I completely stopped all medications, including for heart disease and diabetes, not just the mental health ones. My bipolar symptoms and behavior were not monitored by my family, friends, professionals, or me. I couldn't recognize that anything was wrong. In 2017 and 2018, I would become defensive when a friend or family member even suggested that I might be having mental problems.

In 2020, I was happy most of the time. I was anxious and paranoid about getting the virus, but I wouldn't label my mood as either extreme mania or severe depression. It's easy to conclude that the factors leading to a bipolar manic psychosis were more prevalent in 2017-2018 than in 2020.

What are my chances of having an extreme psychotic breakdown going forward? When would taking my medications regularly, as prescribed, and following my bipolar management plan not be enough? I would expect to have a psychotic episode anytime I experience trauma, especially from the loss of a close family member, as my paternal grandmother did when a train severed her son George's legs.

How will I react to an episode if it happens? I will do as I did when I broke out of the long-term care facility in 2012. I will remember the testimony of Reverend Allen Oggs, the preacher born with cerebral palsy, who wasn't supposed to live. Two of his books, *You Gotta Have the Want-To: A Once in a Lifetime Message* and *You Gotta Get Up Again: It's Worth the Fight*, will be my model.

After all, I have to be around at least until 2040 to see all of my grandchildren graduate from Harvard!

Valediction

When life itself seems lunatic, who knows where madness lies?
Perhaps to be too practical is madness. To surrender dreams—this may be
madness.

Too much sanity may be madness—and maddest of all:
to see life as it is, and not as it should be!

—Miguel de Cervantes Saavedra, *Don Quixote*

On Monday, November 26, 2018, at a residence about five miles from my house, a twenty-three-year-old female, Sierra Duree McCauley, was shot and killed by a twenty-three-year veteran police officer. She was naked and wielded a dangerous seven inch, fixed-blade knife that was originally designed to be used by WW2 military troops. She had cut herself and another individual, and the officer felt threatened. There's been a lot of controversy regarding the use of deadly force in this situation. One law enforcement official said the officer could have felt threatened even had it been a butter knife.

I believe she was experiencing a psychotic episode brought on by some type of mental illness, substance use, trauma, physical illness, or injury. It is sobering to think that could have been me just six months earlier. What if my virtual reality game had included a world that involved the machete in my disaster preparation kit just a few feet away from where I lay on the floor? Had the neighbors not had a key to my house, they might have called the police, who could've found me in a psychotic state with superhuman strength, swinging that machete.

I could have died at least four ways while at home during my severe manic episode—by dehydration, by going into a diabetic coma from low blood glucose levels, by fire, or I could have been killed during a police encounter. It's also amazing that I made it home from Fancy Gap and Bristol before experiencing the most severe parts of my psychotic manic episode. I believe God's divine providence protected me in each of these cases.

I've agonized for forty years, afraid I might hurt a family member, friend, stranger, or even myself. I've been haunted by the accounts of murders committed by those with a mental illness. I was particularly concerned about my children, Megan and Elijah.

During a custody hearing in 1990, Steve's attorney cited a study about mothers with bipolar disorder killing their children, as he repeatedly referred to me as a *maniac depressant* to try to rattle me on the witness stand.

By 1990, I had already had more than eight psychotic breaks. Steve insisted that the custody arrangement ensure that I didn't have the children on two consecutive days, so he could monitor their well-being. The specifics were bizarre. Every other day, every other weekend, every other Thursday night from 7:00 to 9:00 p.m. I've forgotten the rest, but somehow the kids always knew whether to ride the bus or be picked up by car.

Megan says I sometimes forgot and left Elijah and her alone until I came home very late from work. I don't remember that. I felt so flawed and guilty, because my bipolar condition subjected the children to such an abnormal, confining lifestyle.

I was even rebuked by professionals for having children in the first place! How could I have become pregnant with Megan a month after being diagnosed with bipolar disorder? Sure. The chances of my children having the disorder are increased because I have it, but the role of genetics is not definite. When I became pregnant with Elijah, my psychiatrist was insistent that I abort him because of my psychosis after Megan was born. My church's parish nurse once told me I was selfish to have children; people with bipolar disorder should never become parents!

Growing up with a parent who suffers from bipolar disorder can be tough, but Megan and Elijah are resilient. Their elementary school principal called me one night to compliment me because they were so well-adjusted and well-behaved. He said most of the other children in the Banana Split Club, which met weekly to help the kids cope with divorce, frequently got into trouble or caused some kind of disruption.

He didn't see the flip side of the coin, however. There were both positives and negatives of growing up in our households.

I will speak from the perspective of a mother with bipolar disorder. Megan and Elijah would tell me they had three moms: manic mom, depressed mom, and bitch mom. They would sometimes say, "Manic mom, please come out!"

The fact that they felt comfortable saying that is an indication of a lack of boundaries in our relationships. We openly talked about sex and any other topic we might think of.

During the custody proceedings in early 1990, Megan was six and Elijah was four. We saw three court-ordered psychologists for evaluations. One of them told us in front of the children that the divorce was all my fault because I was bipolar. He specifically noted that I didn't set adequate boundaries.

Having a mother with bipolar disorder also impacted my children's social lives. After Megan's middle school friend told her that her parents wouldn't allow her to come to her slumber party because "Her mother is crazy, and she might hurt you," Megan asked me, "Why couldn't you have cancer, or Parkinson's disease, or MS? *Anything* but bipolar disorder! Because if you had one of those, people would understand and try to help us. Nobody understands bipolar disorder!"

But there were many positive benefits of having a manic mom. We would do wild things, like go to my office at 3 a.m., where they would roll from one end of the hall to the other in an office chair with wheels (until a disgruntled, workaholic professor came out of his office and protested). Then we played "Spy" by using our hands as make-believe guns and riding an elevator looking for victims (the missing sibling) on different floors.

There were other benefits, too. I took my aunt and the children to Hawaii for two weeks when they were only five and three. We visited five of the islands—Oahu, Maui, Kauai, Lanai, and Molokai. With Steve's permission, we went to Cancun with my church singles group. Elijah became the group mascot.

After I sold my biotech software company in 1998, we spent three weeks in Florida—one in North Palm Beach (where I took them each summer to visit my aunt), one at a Disney World resort, and one in Key West. There, we stayed in a B&B which moved us from room to room for a reduced price. One night, we got the honeymoon suite with a pink canopy bed. The kids loved that!

Though I was experiencing some level of mania most of the time, I provided enriching training and extracurricular experiences. Megan studied voice and piano, and Elijah played guitar. They both played soccer, learned beginning karate, and did some gymnastics. But they didn't do any of these for more than a year or two. That might have been a function of my problems with focusing.

For the most part, they were happy children. Steve and I had rarely argued or raised our voices when we were married. A few times I swatted them a lick on their tail ends, but they always told Steve when he got home, and he would playfully turn me over his knee and spank me. They mostly thought of me as their older sister. I had no disciplinary authority.

Time-out worked to discipline Elijah, but Megan was too obstinate to follow directions. Once, she'd pestered Elijah all day. I was unable to discipline her, so Elijah took matters into his own hands. He was probably about five. He followed her into her bedroom and called her *fartface*. I have no idea where that came from! I'd never heard the word before. He was precocious, so he probably just made it up.

So I went into the bedroom and asked him, "What did you call her?"

He looked up at me with a scared, but cute, look and stuttered, "Nu-nu-nu nuthin'!"

I replied, "Now Elijah! Tell me the truth! Lying is worse."

So he recanted: "I meant to call her 'Sissy,' but I opened up my mouth and out came 'Fartface!'"

I had to leave the room to keep from laughing.

Megan and Elijah were exposed to entrepreneurship by both parents at an early age. Megan formed her own company, The Drawing Agency, when she was in the second grade. She and the Vice President colored pictures from a coloring book, laminated them with clear contact paper, and sold them to classmates on the playground for a quarter…that is, until the principal discovered it and made them close shop. She'd even made business cards on her dad's MacIntosh without any help.

As an eighth grader, she helped at my company's vendor booth at a Human Genome Conference in Hilton Head, SC. She met lots of people because she held an hourly drawing for nice prizes, like radios and flashlights. The last night of the busy conference, we finally got a chance to stroll down the beach. With everyone we met, it was "Hi, Megan!" No one seemed to know **my** name.

Once on a school snow vacation day, Elijah went to work with me. I was to meet with General Alonzo Short, a three-star general, to discuss potential business collaboration opportunities. After Colin Powell retired, he was the highest ranking African American officer across all branches.

Elijah was about eight or nine years old. We had recently watched the 1990 film *Ghost*, starring Patrick Swayze and Demi Moore.

General Short was way over six feet tall. As he was leaving, he bent his head down to Elijah's eye level, shook his hand, and said, "It was a pleasure to meet you, Elijah!"

Elijah just responded, "Ditto!"

After General Short left my office, I sternly, and probably loudly, said to him: "It's NOT 'ditto!' It's, 'It is a pleasure to meet you too, SIR!'" I wouldn't be surprised if the General heard me, and I can imagine he was smiling.

My children and my business brought me the most joy during those years before I became disabled, around 2000. But bipolar disorder came with its negative sides, which pervaded every aspect of my life.

In addition to the obvious effects on my career and interpersonal relationships, I became the butt of many jokes. If there was a discrepancy between what someone else said and what I said, it was almost always assumed that either I was lying or mistaken because of my bipolar limitations.

During times of hypomania to moderate mania, I would say or do things that caused people to reject me. Many times, I didn't know what I'd done. They wouldn't answer my calls, emails, or letters of apology. Once I got a *Return to Sender, Address Unknown* letter back from a childhood friend I'd known since before the first grade! For real! We'd reconnected and had been hanging out for a few months. For another friend, who'd been especially close, I figured out what I'd said inadvertently after I hadn't seen her for about twelve years.

Lost friends were probably justified in severing the relationship, especially if it was a romantic one. Once I became manic and sent letters or emails to about seventy-five people asking them to forgive me. I had contacted them because of the power of suggestion. My pastor had recommended the Sunday before that we contact someone that week with whom we needed to reconcile. My mania went overboard! Many responded that I had never done anything wrong that they knew about. A few didn't respond at all. I also got some very negative responses.

I feel remorse about the broken relationships and friendships. I always wanted a golden-wedding-anniversary type of marriage, but my first one lasted twelve years and the second only eight. Each husband sued ME for divorce. It's not surprising, since it's been estimated that about ninety percent of marriages end in divorce, if one or both partners has bipolar disorder.[5]

Bipolar disorder affected my spiritual life as well. I wish I had a nickel for every time my personal relationship with Christ has been questioned, usually because of my sensuality and poor judgment. As if that's not enough to shake my Christian faith, some have taken it to another whole level and labeled me as demon-possessed. And many times I've been guilty of drinking the Kool-Aid, especially when I'm fragile and feeling vulnerable.

I have so many unanswered questions about the causes of my delusions during a psychotic episode that I've fallen for this one sometimes. How can I think I'm Jesus or Mary or another Biblical character when many other people have the same delusions, if we aren't controlled by the same demon(s)? Why do my times of superhuman strength resemble the portrayal of Legion as the demoniac of the Gerasenes/Gadarenes region in three passages of the New Testament in the Christian Bible (Matthew 8:28-34; Mark 5:1-20; Luke 8:26-39)?

After my 2018 severe manic episode with psychosis, fear of demon possession raised its ugly head again. I've studied many Christian writers, including Dr. Billy Graham, all of whom say that a Christian can't be completely taken over and controlled by demons. While demons can influence Christians, the Holy Spirit lives within us, and no demon can take His place inside us. But it continues to be hurtful to be called Legion.

I'm often asked if I'm fearful of my future. In particular, do I think I'd ever commit suicide? The National Institute of Mental Health (NIMH) reports that as many as one in five patients with bipolar disorder completes suicide[6].

The few times I've had suicidal thoughts, I see in my mind the psychiatrist who, years ago, got right in my face and said, "If you commit

---

[5] Hara Estroff Marano, "Managing Bipolar Disorder," *Psychology Today*, November 1, 2003.
[6]https://www.ncbi.nlm.nih.gov/pmc/articles/PMC6723289/

suicide, your children will NEVER get over it!" Then I think of the friends who've lost a parent or spouse, and I feel their reactions. In one case, a man with twelve children told me about their mother shooting herself in front of all of them on Christmas Day. What a tragedy! These remembrances snap me right out of any suicidal thoughts!

I'm also fortunate to have family members in addition to my children who love and support me. My older brother recently said, "I've known you for over sixty years. Many times I don't understand the things you say and do. I will never understand bipolar disorder, but I love you unconditionally."

And my cousin Karen once told me that while praying for me, she felt God was telling her to tell me that HE UNDERSTANDS BIPOLAR DISORDER and my conflicting behavior that often randomly oscillates between piety and hedonism, especially during elevated states of mania.

God is merciful and forgiving. Even though I have often rebelled against Him, His Grace is sufficient for me. (2 Corinthians 12:9)

Betty, my dear friend and spiritual mentor, once asked me, "Are you bitter about your health problems and subsequent life experiences?" I told her, "No! I've always believed an angel told me when I was three that someday I would be able to help a lot of people."

And **THIS IS IT!**

No great mind has ever existed without a touch of madness.

—Aristotle

The End

ACKNOWLEDGMENTS

Writing *When Brilliance and Madness Collide* has been an adventure filled with challenges and disappointments, as well as exhilaration and a deep sense of accomplishment and self-fulfillment. The encouragement and support of many individuals and professionals kept me going during critical junctures.

I want to express my sincere appreciation to:

My family, for their unwavering support, understanding, and patience during this ambitious endeavor. Special recognition is given to my son, John Manning, MD, for writing the Foreword and providing significant contributions and assistance throughout the entire process. Jeff Watson, my son-in-law, who gave feedback on writing style and content. I am grateful and want to commend my children for their endurance and resilience during my bipolar journey. I'm so proud of who they've become, both personally and professionally.

My best friend, James H. Cox, whose words of support and belief in me kept me motivated during times of self-doubt.

My friend and adviser, Catherine Hiller, PhD, an accomplished author who has published two children's books, a memoir, and several novels, and a story collection, which earned her praise from John Updike. She gave me detailed reviews of earlier drafts and suggested many ideas for substantive changes. She was expecting a memoir and thought I should write about my personal and professional achievements. I compromised and added the section "My Wild Ride."

My mentor, friend, and creative writing instructor, Don Williams, whose guidance and wisdom have been instrumental in shaping my ideas and honing my writing skills. Don is also an accomplished and recognized author. He read an early draft and offered beneficial instruction. He has stood beside and encouraged me all the way.

My therapist, Dr. Lisa Bridgewater, who encouraged me during late 2020 to start writing again after reviewing a draft I wrote between mid-2018 and mid-2019. She provided valuable input as a mental health professional by reading later versions of the manuscript and offering numerous excellent suggestions. By the end of 2021, the manuscript draft was nearly complete.

My brilliant developmental editor, Deborah K. Steinberg, who rearranged the original text in 2022 and made recommendations that helped transform this book into its present publishable form. She also wrote the Prologue and found the opening line somewhere in the middle of the original manuscript that immediately grabs the reader's attention and propels the story forward. Thank you, Deborah, for all of your hard work.

John's "other" parents, Bob and Joy Sutton, who read *When Brilliance and Madness Collide* from the unique perspective of having taken him under their wings and caring for him like a son during some of the most difficult years of my bipolar life experiences.

My new friend, Dick Nash, who asked to read the manuscript after overhearing me discuss it with some other friends. Much to my surprise, he finished reading it in just a few days and provided me with excellent feedback.

My mentor, Betty Maples, who has guided my spiritual growth for nearly four decades. Her daughters, Melanie Harris and Maria Maples, MD, have assisted my family when we needed help, as if they were my own daughters.

My dear friend, Shirley Bohanan, who read one of my personal essays in 2016 and recommended I write a book. She's encouraged me throughout this journey and motivated me to never give up!

The National Alliance on Mental Illness (NAMI), which invited me to submit an Express Talk for NAMICon 2023, titled "Avoiding Transference for Mental Health Behavior."

Special thanks to the team at Parson's Porch Books, especially David Russell Tullock, for their skill, commitment, and enthusiasm in bringing this book to life. Throughout this publishing process, David has shown compassion, patience, and support.

I am grateful for everyone who has been a part of my wild ride.

APPENDIX

Glossary of Medical Terms and Abbreviations

affect

Patient's immediate expression of emotion; affect is what you feel, and emotion is a reaction to your feelings. Affect ranges from broad (or full), restricted (or constricted), blunted (or flat), and labile.

—*broad*: typical affect expected of the average person

—*restricted*: range and intensity of emotional response is not as intense as normally expected; common in depression, inhibited personalities, and schizophrenia

—*blunted*: virtually no outward evidence of any emotion; characterized by diminished facial expressions, less eye contact, using fewer gestures and other body language to express emotion, speaking in a dull, flat voice, and may have trouble understanding emotions of other people

—*labile*: intense and sudden positive or negative changes in emotion (mood swings) that are not caused by a physiological condition or substance; either display emotions excessively or show inappropriate emotions in specific situations (for example, laughing or smiling at a funeral or other sad occasion)

A/P

Assessment/Plan Such as, if a patient is awaiting psychiatric placement

ataxia

Poor muscle control that causes clumsy, voluntary movements. May cause difficulty with balance and walking, hand coordination, speech and swallowing, and eye movements.

AV or AVHs	**A**uditory/**V**isual **H**allucinations are the phenomenon of hearing sounds that others do not hear or seeing things that others do not see
CABG	**C**oronary **A**rtery **B**ypass **G**raft heart surgery
chlorpromazine	Generic name for Thorazine
CNA	Certified Nursing Assistant or nurse aide
CT Scan	**C**omputed **T**omography scan; a series of detailed pictures of areas inside the body made by a computer linked to an x-ray machine
CXR	Chest x-ray
ECG or EKG	Electrocardiogram: records the electrical signal from the heart to check for certain heart conditions
EMS	Emergency Medical Services
ER	Emergency Room
euthymic mood	Feeling relatively neutral; not extremely happy or sad
HCC	**H**ierarchical **C**ondition **C**ategory coding
HPI	**H**istory of **P**resent **I**llness
IV	Intravenous: administered into a vein(s)
lamotrigine	Generic name for Lamictal
lithium	Generic name for Lithobid or Eskalith
olanzapine	or (OLANZapine) Generic name for Zyprexa
po (per os)	By mouth

pressured speech	A tendency to speak rapidly and frenziedly, motivated by an urgency that may not be apparent. May feel like you can't stop. Might jump from one idea to the next. People could have trouble following the conversation.
	Pressured speech can be rapid, difficult to interrupt, erratic, irrelevant, or too tangential for the listener to understand. Often a sign of mania or hypomania.
PRN or prn	Use medication "as needed."
Pt	Medical patient
qhs	Daily at bedtime; "q" standing for "quaque" and the "h" indicating the number of hours
quetiapine	Generic name for Seroquel
ROS	Review of systems
SI	Suicidal ideation
SI/HI	Suicidal ideation/homicidal ideation
tangential speech	Verbal communication that repeatedly diverges from the original subject to random, irrelevant ideas and topics, resulting from disorganized thought processes or a diminished ability to focus attention. A person might start telling a story, but burdens the story with so much irrelevant detail that they never get to the point or the conclusion.
TD or TDK	Tardive Dyskinesia is a movement disorder characterized by uncontrollable, sudden, irregular, abnormal, and repetitive movements of the face, torso, and/or other body parts. It can develop as a side effect of the prolonged use of a medication, most commonly, antipsychotic drugs.

181

triage	Preliminary assessment of the urgency and nature of medical treatment required
vital signs	Body temperature, pulse rate, respiration rate, blood pressure
VSS	**Vital Signs Stable**
x3	Oriented to person (know who they are), place (where they are) and time (what day it is)
x4	Oriented to x3 (person, place, and time) plus awareness of situation (what just happened to you)